# Confessions
of an
*irritable*
mother

# Confessions
## of an
# *irritable*
# mother

**hope** for
overwhelmed
moms

k a r e n   h o s s i n k

PSALM 115:1, LLC.

# Confessions of an
# irritable
# mother

**hope** for overwhelmed moms

All Scripture quotations are taken from the Holy Bible, New International Version®. NIV. Copyright © 1973, 1978, 1984 by International Bible Society. Used by permission of Zondervan Publishing House. All rights reserved.

ISBN-13: 978-0-9786731-0-9
ISBN-10: 0-9786731-0-7
Library of Congress Control Number 2006905451

Cover Design:
**Michael Cox, Alpha Advertising**
Sidell, Illinois
www.AlphaAdvertising.com

Book Layout & Interior Design:
**Suzette Perry, Infinity Graphics**
Okemos, Michigan
www.InfinityGraphics.com

Printer:
**Data Reproductions**
Auburn Hills, Michigan
www.DataRepro.com

Web site Design:
**Pam Laing, PSL Designs**
Canton, Michigan
www.PSLDesigns.com

Copyediting:
**Christine Schapp**
Rockford, Michigan
www.PathPartners.com

**Published by:**
**Psalm 115:1, LLC**
**Lansing, MI 48912**

www.IrritableMother.com

*To my children, Elizabeth, Joshua, and Matthew*

*I lovingly dedicate this book to you.*
*I am honored that God has chosen to bless my life with each of you*
*and I pray that I may reflect His love to you every day.*

# Acknowledgements

A book is never written without the loving support of a team of people. I want to give a special thanks to the individuals that helped guide me on this journey:

- To Kay Arthur, Jerry Bridges, and Kathy Troccoli — for playing a significant role in my journey toward holiness. I am forever grateful for the ministry that each of you has.

- To Tammy and Nikki — for sharing your lives and stories. You have both been blessings to me. I love seeing how God has worked in each of you!

- To my beloved mentor, Jenni — for your friendship and support. God truly speaks His love to me through you. Maybe someday I'll let you read through my journal and you can see how many times I've spontaneously written, "Thank You for bringing Jenni into my life!" I am so glad that He brought us together. Thanks for sharing your story with me and my readers.

- To my small group, Amber, Jason, Chris and Dawn — for your support and encouragement throughout the process of this book. You celebrated with me and believed in me. I love you guys!

- To my prayer partner and fellow Irritable Mother, Melissa — for cheering me on and praying for me as I've been on this journey. I love you. I wish you didn't have to move, but we know that God is good and He has blessed me by allowing our paths to cross for a short season.

➤ To my prayer team — for faithfully bringing me and this project before the throne of God. Your support, faith, and words of encouragement mean so much to me!

➤ To my editor and book coach, Christine Schaap — for your honesty, even when you were hesitant to say what you really thought. I'm glad you did! You have drawn me out and this book will bear fruit because of your guidance and words of wisdom. I am so thankful that God allowed our paths to cross!

➤ To my wonderful, wise, loving, sexy husband, Brian — for loving me through the fire. I appreciate your words of wisdom and grace. Thank you for understanding me (as much as is possible!) and for supporting me and dreaming with me throughout the process of writing this book. God blessed me beyond measure when He brought you into my life.

➤ To my Lord and my God — without You and Your work in my life, I would have nothing of worth to say. Thank You for giving me a story. Thank You for allowing me to be a part of Your plan and for the opportunities You have given me to share about Your goodness. I want to be an instrument You use for Your glory!

# Table of Contents

# *Introduction*

I REMEMBER THE FIRST TIME I considered public speaking. I had just been to a TimeOut for Women! conference and I thought, "Wouldn't it be cool to be one of those speakers!" And that was about as far as my thought went.

It was probably a year or two later, when I began to understand God was using my children to shape me, that the idea of speaking entered my mind a second time. I thought, "When I have a better understanding of what God is doing, maybe I'll see if I can share about it at MOPS." [MOPS International is a network of local groups that provides support for mothers of children from infancy through kindergarten.]

Time went on and God did reveal Himself more clearly to me. I was beginning to understand God was using my children to transform me, and my heart was beginning to ache for other moms who were burdened. I wanted them to know this hope God had given me.

I heard a speaker say the intersection of what breaks God's heart and what breaks our own heart is probably the area He's calling us to ministry. I wondered, "God, do You want me to go somewhere with this message?"

What clinched it for me was a meeting with my mentor, Jenni. She asked me, "What really drives you? Where is your passion?" It was in reflecting on those questions that I became clear about what I wanted to do. God had given me hope and a story to share, and I wanted to share it. So I began making contacts with people I knew from MOPS and they connected me with other MOPS groups and I started sharing my story.

Just having the opportunity to speak to groups of moms at MOPS meetings would have been enough for me. I love how God can take the hard times we have gone through and use them to encourage and give hope to others. If my ministry never went any further than reaching out to moms around Lansing, Michigan, it really would have been okay with me.

However, as women talked with me after meetings and told me how encouraged they were by my story, I longed to share *more*. Not just more often, but more of my story. Really, though, how much could I share in 45-50 minutes? That desire, coupled with a few other promptings, led me to pursue writing this book.

God is so amazing. Just a year ago I was getting serious about finding speaking opportunities. Now He has me writing a book. I love it!

When I was searching for a way to organize this book, I saw in my mind three distinct "parts" to my story and tried to come up with three words which would encompass each part. Then one day, it hit me. Since I use the image of refining silver as the centerpiece of my talk, why not take the whole process — the mining, the preparation, and the refining — as the framework for my book?

It made sense to me as I considered how those steps are so like what God has done in my life. First, He mined my soul, retrieving something which wasn't very attractive at the time, but that He knew had value. Next, He prepared me for refining by teaching me to trust in Him and the work He was going to do. Now, He is refining me, continually making me more like Jesus by holding me in the Refiner's fire so my impurities can burn away. To help you see the connection, I have included a brief description of each of the ancient processes at the beginning of each section.

I have also provided Reflection Questions at the end of each chapter. Please use them for personal reflection, or to help spark discussion if you're reading this book with a group. If you don't already have a journal, perhaps you can start one now and spend time writing out your answers to the questions. I'll admit, sometimes I'm so interested in reading a book that I blow right past the questions and start reading the next chapter. While I hope you are eager to keep reading, my greater desire is for you to spend time absorbing and processing the message, letting God speak to you.

As I've been writing this book, I have been praying for you. My hope and prayer is three-fold: I pray that (1) you will grow in your love for God, (2) your desire to pursue holiness will increase, and (3) you will be convinced of God's goodness in everything.

Perhaps you are an "irritable mother" and can relate to every frustration I share. Maybe your source of tension is something else, another relationship, or a different stressor altogether. Whoever and wherever you are, I pray that God in His sovereignty and loving kindness will meet you in the pages of this book and will draw you closer to Himself.

## PART I

# The Mining

*"For a miner must have the greatest of skill in his work,*
*that he may know first of all what mountain or hill, what valley or plain,*
*can be prospected most profitably, or what he should leave alone."*[1]

When prospecting for silver, a miner needed to first consider the location of his digging. What was the condition of the terrain? What was the condition of nearby roads and waterways? Did someone already have claim to the land? Once the miner determined that mining the land would be profitable, he could set to work building his mine, digging the shafts and tunnels.[2]

Within the mines, ore was extracted by several methods. Some rock crumbled easily and required only a pick to be dislodged from the wall. Other rock needed to be chiseled out with a hammer and one of various iron tools, depending on its hardness. Still other rock, which was too hard to break with tools, was shattered by fire.[3]

*~ Chapter One ~*

# The Meanest Mom in the World

IT WAS A SIMPLE ASSIGNMENT. It should have been easy for me to do. I was participating in the Apples of Gold mentoring program at my church and we were doing Lesson Three: Loving Your Children. Our first assignment was to "Take a look at a favorite photograph of each of your children. What do you love most about each child?"

Simple? Yes.

Easy? Not for me.

And I felt terrible.

I had given birth to three beautiful children: Elizabeth, Joshua and Matthew. I had nursed each of them for a year. I had caressed their silky skin, tickled their pudgy legs, and sang to and danced with them for hours.

Now I sat with a book on my lap, a pen in my hand, and their pictures at my side. I was stumped. I couldn't think of what to write down, what I loved most, about Joshua.

How could that be? What kind of mother was I?

That answer was easy: *"The Meanest Mom in the World!"* At least that's what Joshua told me. Every day. Several times.

I still remember one summer day outside with Joshua. He and I were in the middle of a spat. I wanted him to go inside and put away his toys and he didn't want to. He stormed off in another direction ranting and raving about me being the *Meanest Mom in the World.*

When I went into the house, the phone was ringing. As I picked up the receiver and said, "Hello?" a kind voice on the other end said to me, "You're *not* the Meanest Mom in the World!" It was my neighbor, Amy. She had heard the entire exchange and was calling to give me encouragement. Thanks, Amy!

## How did it happen?

I didn't start off mean. And certainly, being the *Meanest Mom in the World* was never my goal. Yet, somehow, my son thought I was worthy of the title. To be fair, the majority of times Joshua crowned me queen of the meanies was when I was punishing him, or when I wasn't giving him what he wanted. Nonetheless, he seemed pretty convinced I deserved the title and when you hear something often enough, you start to believe it's true.

But how did it happen?

I started off so tender and loving. When I was first pregnant, I thought I was going to give birth to angels and I, myself, was going to be angelic. I was going to do everything just right. I read all the books. I knew "what to expect" when I was expecting *and* during the first year. I made homemade baby wipes. I vowed to let no processed sugar pass my baby's lips during her first year. (Okay, that one only held true for the first baby.) I made special concoctions to treat diaper rash. I was even going to be environmentally friendly and use cloth diapers. (Uh, that didn't last either.) We spent lots of time reading, singing, and playing games to build skills and brainpower. I wanted to be perfect.

Occasionally, a few "older and wiser" women would try to offer me advice or suggestions, but I secretly didn't think I needed it. After all, I had read the books. How hard could this mothering thing be? I was sure I could handle it — *perfectly.*

So what happened? My babies grew up and started expressing their own wills and opinions and I found out I wasn't perfect.

They made and left behind messes — toys and crumbs and spilled milk — and I got tired of cleaning them up. My kids decided sharing wasn't fun and fought with each other instead, and I grew impatient trying to maintain order. They wanted more and more of me while I, on the other hand, just wanted to run away.

When things were stressful, I tried to remain under control, but I usually ended up yelling at someone. When demands were high, I began to snap.

To be sure, I loved my kids and had wonderful times with them. Moments came though when the stress got to me, when I felt overwhelmed, when I started yelling, when Joshua thought I was the *Meanest Mom in the World.* It was in those moments that I despaired of being a mother.

I remember once when I felt like each of my kids was relentlessly pursuing me with, "I want," "Will you?" "Give me," "That isn't fair," "He's hitting me." I couldn't handle it anymore and I retreated from them. I shut myself outside the kitchen and sat on the step weeping. I wanted so desperately to be a good mom — to meet their needs and do everything just right — but I sat there completely overwhelmed.

Tears flooded my eyes as I honestly questioned God's wisdom in giving me children. Certainly I knew in my head that God is all-wise, but it really seemed to me that I couldn't handle this mothering thing. I wondered if maybe, just this once, He may have made a mistake.

What happened to the angels I was going to have? This wasn't what I was expecting. *The books didn't tell me I was going to have days like these!*

Have you ever been in this position? Have you been at your wits' end with your kids? Have you felt like a complete failure as a mother — like you're in way over your head? Have you wondered how you'll ever make it through? Please know that *you are not alone.*

To help you deal with the times when you're feeling this way, I have created for you The Irritable Mother's Survival Kit. ***For a free copy visit my website: www.IrritableMother.com.***

## I'm not alone

I met Tammy when I was speaking to a MOPS group. She has two sons, and although her children haven't named her "The Meanest Mom in the World," she has dealt with issues of anger as a mother.

Tammy told me before she had children, people described her as laid back and always smiling. They would comment, "Tammy never gets mad." Her first baby didn't change things much. She still felt as though she could handle things. She still felt "in control."

"Initially, mothering was everything I'd hoped it would be and more," says Tammy. "But after I had my second child, everything changed. I started reacting to life in a way I never expected. I always assumed I would be a patient mother who would only get a little frustrated once in awhile. I never dreamed that I would get as angry as I have with my boys! I was doing such a wonderful job raising Justin that I thought it would be a piece of cake to have another child. *Wrong!* I discovered how much of a control freak I was whenever things didn't go my way."

Tammy shared with me that she would get angry when she was tired or under stress. When her boys got a little older and sibling rivalry set in, she found herself yelling more. At times, she became so angry she began to feel physically sick.

Eventually, her anger began to dissipate. She learned to recognize which things triggered her fury and worked to avoid them. Instead of dealing with what she calls "extreme anger," she stepped down to "crabbiness." She just has "those kind of days" now and then. But this progress didn't happen before Tammy went through a significant time of discouragement.

She prayed and studied her Bible, but didn't see any change. When she shared about her anger with other moms she received sympathy, but no one admitted they had similar struggles. So she remained confused and frustrated, wondering what was wrong with her.

God had blessed her with two adorable little boys. Why was she having such a hard time? Just like I had, Tammy at times wondered if God may have made a mistake in making her a mother.

## Are you kidding?

I have often been "consoled" by others — usually by mothers of grown children who seemed to have a different view of these times. Frequently when my children and I are experiencing a struggle of some sort, one of these older women will say in the kindest of voices, "Oh, they grow up so fast, dear! There will be a time when you'll miss these days."

Have you heard that line? I don't know what has clouded their memories! Though I've never actually said it to anyone, I have *thought*, "You don't really remember what these days are like, do you?" Call me crazy, but there are several of "these days" that I can't imagine missing.

I remember a conversation I had once with the father of a teen-age boy. I was sharing with him about a particular struggle I was having with Joshua who was five at the time. The father essentially told me to "take heart." He told me he'd gone through similar things, but now his son, at thirteen, was a totally different kid and so much easier. I thought, "Oh, so you're telling me I only have *eight more years* of this. Great. Thanks for the encouragement!"

Now, I know these people mean well. And what they're saying is probably true. At the time, however, my thinking was more like, "I'm not living 'in eight years.' I'm living today, and I'm struggling today, and I need help *now!*"

The help I needed came in an unexpected way.

## Reflection Questions:

1. How is mothering, in reality, different from what you imagined it to be?

2. Have you ever been called, "the meanest mom in the world," or something equivalent? How did it make you feel?

3. Have you ever questioned God's wisdom?

## Chapter Two

# New Hope

**THE LEAVES WERE CHANGING THEIR COLOR.** It was the middle of September and time for my annual date with my mother-in-law. Every September since 1997 has found the two of us at the TimeOut for Women! conference in Grand Rapids, Michigan. And, boy, did I need a time out!

What a gift that day was to me. It was a whole day away from real life. I had a whole day to enjoy friends, to listen to great speakers, to sing praises to God, and to hear from Him without interruption or distraction. I really needed to be there.

When I go to events like TimeOut, God never ceases to amaze me. Thousands of women come, each one with her own story, her own hurts, and her own needs. Each one comes, as I do, needing a touch from her Maker and He delivers. We're all hearing the same speakers, but God uses them to speak to each one of us individually.

On that day, the message I heard from each woman who addressed us was this: Joshua was a gift from God to me. He was a blessing. God didn't give me Joshua to punish me or to make me miserable. Though the conference wasn't about "mothering," that's where I was, that's what I needed, and that's where God met me.

The message God had for me wasn't earth shaking. No fireworks went off at the conclusion of the conference, and I didn't drive off happily ever after into the sunset. In fact, in my head I already knew *all* of my children are a gift from God. No major revelation there. What spoke to me was His gentle persistence as He reminded me through one speaker after another that Joshua was a gift. It was as if He were saying to me, **"Trust Me, Karen. I'm in this situation. It is for your good."**

I didn't drive off into the sunset that day, but I did drive off with an overwhelming sense of *hope*.

## Beginning a new work

As I have reflected back, I have come to the conclusion it was at the TimeOut conference that God began a new work in me. I didn't wake up the next morning with a halo shining around my head. "Mother of the Year" awards did not loom on my horizon. I was still no match for June Cleaver or Mary Poppins. God had kindled something in me, though, and I was eager to learn more.

Up until then I had considered my station in life, being a mother of young children, as a season. And seasons pass. Living in Michigan I see this passage all the time. Even the weatherman jokes, "If you don't like the weather, just wait five minutes. It will change!" I know what to do when it gets really bad: you just take a deep breath and grab an extra sweater or turn on the sprinkler and tell yourself relief will come eventually.

In regards to my children, many times I had the attitude that I just needed to keep plugging along and press on to the day when it would be all over. Sure, there would be times when I would simply need to grin and bear it, but it was only for a season. One day my children would be grown and I would be finished, so I thought. Although my mom tells me it *never* ends!

Thinking about my children with a sense of hope, however, I began to see things differently. I realized when this season passes, my children aren't the only ones who will have grown up. Yes, they are changing and learning new things every day. Yes, I have an important role to play in their passage to adulthood. But I was becoming aware that just as my children are changing, so too, *I* will not be the same on the other side of mothering.

So my hope was increasing. I was confident my children were gifts from God. They were blessings. Not only was I alert to the blessing, but I was growing in awareness that being a mother was going to bring about change in me, too. Yet, the awareness still left me with the sense I needed to *wait* for good things. That is to say, it seemed to me when my kids were grown and out on their own, when they weren't home whining and fighting and begging, when my work as a mother of young children was "done," *then and only then* would I would experience peace and joy.

It seemed to me the good stuff was at the end and I would need to *endure* the means to the end, rather than to *enjoy* it. Have you ever felt this way? Hold that thought! I'll talk more about it later.

## One more step

After some time passed, God began to stir in me in a different way. I was at a women's conference when it started. Kathy Troccoli was the speaker and she talked about being a holy woman. She said being a Christian woman isn't the same thing as being a holy woman, and was urging us to pursue holiness. At the time, I didn't fully grasp this calling and I wanted to know more. I knew I didn't want to sit under a label. I needed to be real.

Be real? That was a scary thought. People knew me as a "nice Christian woman." I was active in church — as a greeter, nursery worker, Sunday school teacher, small group leader, and MOPS steering team member. What would people think if they knew I blew up at my kids? Would they still like me if they knew I wasn't in the running for "Mother of the Year?" I wanted to appear like I had it all together. But I didn't. For me, "together" simply wasn't "real."

I remember one Sunday morning when we were singing, "The Heart of Worship" in church. God's presence was so real to me and I was praying the words as I sang them.

> *I'll bring you more than a song*
> *For a song in itself*
> *Is not what You have required*
> *You search much deeper within*
> *Through the way things appear*
> *You're looking into my heart*[1]

Oh, the thought of God looking into my heart! I stood there before Him, weeping. I wanted my heart to be a good place for Him to look. I wanted Him to be pleased with what He saw. Yet in my struggles with my kids, I felt so ugly.

When the service ended, I went to the front of the sanctuary to receive prayer. I told the women who would pray for me about my desire to have a heart which is pleasing to God. I told them about my struggles with my children and that I wanted to change. They talked with me about seeking holiness, and then they prayed for me. I was encouraged by their words and hopeful God was working in me.

Do you see yourself in any of these descriptions? Do you struggle between being "real" and being what you think people expect of you? If you struggle with this as well, I want to encourage you to stick with me because God has great things in store for us.

# A call to holiness

A few months later, it was time for another date with my mother-in-law. I was on my way to TimeOut, and God was waiting for me there. As always, the speakers were wonderful, godly women and I was delighted to hear them all. God used two of them in particular, however, to grab hold of me tightly: Kathy Troccoli and Kay Arthur.

As when I'd heard her before, Kathy talked about holiness. God had been stirring this desire in my heart and I was drawn to what she was saying. I was starting to understand that to be "Christian" is to be saved, but to be "holy" is to be sanctified.

I knew I was saved. That event occurred during my freshman year at Western Michigan University when I realized simply going to church wasn't what I needed to have a relationship with God. I had grown up attending church every Sunday with the exception of those rare times I convinced my mom I was too tired to get up. I sang in the choir, faithfully attended church camp every summer and knew the basic Bible stories. As far as I was concerned, I was good to go. Surely I had done more good than bad in my life. I believed in God and even prayed before dinner and bedtime. I thought those things made me a Christian.

During my first year of college, however, I came to understand that going to church, knowing the stories, and even believing in God weren't enough. I needed to recognize my need of a Savior, to come to terms with the truth that I was a sinful woman who deserved to spend eternity separated from a holy God.

Understanding my condition, I needed to place my faith in the One who came from heaven to earth to live a perfect life and die on a cross so I could be forgiven. Through Jesus' death and resurrection the way was made for me, for all of us, to be reconciled to God. And during my freshman year of college I asked Jesus to come into my life, to forgive my sins, and to make a place for me in heaven.

What did it mean, though, to be sanctified? According to Webster's Dictionary, to be sanctified is "to be set apart to a sacred purpose, to be purified." A look into some Bible dictionaries reveals, "our sanctification has to do with God's transformation of us into persons whose actions in daily life are expressions of the Lord."[2] Another resource states that sanctification is, "the process by which an entity is brought into relationship with or attains the likeness of the holy."[3] More simply put, when God sanctifies us, when He makes us holy, He is making us more like Jesus.

At the moment of our salvation, we are forgiven of our sins and granted eternal life, but God doesn't want to stop there. He is only beginning. If we will cooperate with Him, He will make us holy. God's Spirit will take up residence within us and transform us into His likeness.

At the end of the conference, Kathy invited Kay back to the platform to address us one more time, which is when God closed His grip on me. Kay was passionate about calling us to pursue God. She urged us to know Him and His word, to allow Him to transform us and make us holy. Oh, how I felt His call and wanted to answer.

An invitation was given then to come to the altar and pray, to lay ourselves at the foot of the cross. When I went forward, Kay was sitting on the steps and I went over to her and asked her to pray for me. I told her I was already a Christian but I wanted to be holy, and she prayed for me. Though she didn't know me, I could sense her love for me in the Lord and I was blessed. I knew God was present, was hearing her prayer, and was going to work in me.

I didn't want that moment to end. I wanted to stay with all those women, basking in the presence of God. I wanted Kathy to keep singing. I wanted to pour myself out to God, but the conference had ended and it was time to return to my life.

Oh, no, it wasn't! I had encountered God, and I could never "return" to the life I'd been leading. I would never be the same.

## Out of the Mines

And that, as I see it, was the end of my mining process. Though my exterior was rough and the beauty was hidden, God saw something of value in me and He went after it. Sometimes He was able to delicately tap on me, and other times I think I was more like the hardest rocks which required fire to shatter them so they could be taken out of the mine and prepared for refining.

As I reflect on this part of my journey, I am amazed at God's wisdom and care for me. I am thankful He was willing to "descend into the mines" of my soul to pick, to dig, to blast, whatever was necessary to bring me to the place where He could transform me. He knew what was needed and He did it.

I believe the same God who mined the silver from my soul is intimately interested in the silver resting in your soul, too.

Do you believe there is something of value to God deep within you? Perhaps there are times when you feel ugly — when your kids say they don't like you and you find yourself agreeing with them — and you can't imagine how God could possibly have any interest in you at all. In spite of those times, I pray God will give you hope that there is something beautiful in you and that He is working to reveal it.

## Reflection Questions:

1. To what extent do you relate to the idea that when your kids are grown up, then you'll finally be able to experience peace and joy?

2. What does it mean to you to be real? Is it hard for you to be real?

3. Have you ever considered the difference between being a "Christian" and being "holy"?

4. Where do you think you are in your journey toward holiness? Have you ever thought about it before? Is it something you'd like to pursue? Or something you've been seeking for quite a while?

# PART II

# The Preparation

*"Although the miners, in the shafts or tunnels,*
*have sorted over the material which they mine,*
*still the ore which has been broken down and carried out*
*must be broken into pieces by a hammer or minutely crushed,*
*so that the more valuable and better parts can be*
*distinguished from the inferior and worthless portions."*[1]

After the silver had been mined, but before it was refined, it went through a time of preparation. Large chunks were broken into smaller pieces and sorted. Smaller pieces were crushed into a powder and further sorted. Some of the ore was burned first, in order to make it soft enough to break apart.[2] The ore was then washed and poured through a series of screens to separate out even more of the rock and earth from the silver.[3]

While each of these processes was necessary to prepare the silver for refining, there was still another important step to finish the preparation. This process was known as smelting. In smelting, the ore was placed in a furnace and heated until it melted. When the ore melted, the earth and pebbles that rose to the surface were skimmed off and cast aside. This process was repeated until nothing further could be extracted from the silver.[4] At this point, the molten silver was allowed to cool into a cake and was ready to be refined.

*⤜ Chapter Three ⤝*

# You Can Trust Me

I TRULY CAN'T REMEMBER if someone at TimeOut suggested it or if God brought it to my mind some other way, but after the conference I decided I wanted to find a mentor. Somewhere out there, I knew there must be a woman who loved God passionately and who could pour some of that love into me. I wanted to find someone who would help me draw closer to Him, who could help me understand what it means to be holy and who could encourage me through this journey.

Before we go any further, I want to clearly plant this thought in your mind: *If you don't already have a mentor in your life, find her!* Pray for her. Seek her out. Ask about a mentoring program at your church. Watch for a woman who seems to be oozing the love of God and approach her. We weren't meant to travel this road alone, and a mentor is a great person with whom you can travel.

I have heard it said God gives us "grace with faces," that is, people who can be His grace to us, who can help us get through the difficult days and soar through the good ones. I believe it. Who knows? Maybe someday you will be able to turn around and be a mentor to someone else!

## "Before they call I will answer"

I was sitting alone in my dining room one afternoon contemplating God and my desire for holiness when my phone rang. It was Cathy, the Director of Women's Ministries at my church. When she asked, "How are you?" I decided to skip the usual, "Fine, thanks. How are you?" and answered her honestly. I told her about the journey on which God was leading me, about my desire to be holy, and about my wish for a mentor.

God is so amazing. Cathy told me she had just been talking with some people about beginning a mentoring program! She wanted to find some women in the church who would come along side younger women and build into their lives. Putting this program together would take a few months, but Cathy asked if I would like to be a part of it when it was ready. Oh, yes!

Isaiah 65:24 says, "Before they call I will answer; while they are still speaking I will hear." Don't you love that? Although we are not always privy to His work, though sometimes He seems hidden and maybe it seems like He isn't doing anything at all, He answers before we call and hears while we are still speaking. Imagine, the Creator of the universe knows your heart and exactly what you need, and whether or not you are aware of it, He is orchestrating life just the way it should be for you!

God was at work bringing me into a mentoring relationship before I even knew I wanted one. Although I was going to have to wait for a little while, I was sure God would bring it to pass, and I was delighted.

## In the midst of the struggle

In the mean time, God was not putting my life and my journey toward holiness on hold. At the time I didn't recognize it, but my struggle with my kids was an integral part of the journey. And I was definitely struggling.

It seemed like my kids wanted *so much* of me. And didn't they deserve it? After all, I *am* their mother! So often, though, I felt smothered, like I just wanted a way out, some of my own air to breathe. I struggled with knowing where to put boundaries so that I would have time for myself.

I would sometimes sugarcoat selfishness and call it "necessary" time for me, or for household chores. For instance, if my daughter wanted me to play a game I didn't want to play, I would say I needed to read a book. Or if one of my sons wanted me to read *their* book and I didn't want to, I might say I needed to fold the laundry. While alone time and chores are legitimate needs, I know I was using them as excuses for not doing things the kids wanted.

After a time, guilt would set in and then I would do the thing they wanted. Yes, I'd do it, but often begrudgingly or with every intention of getting "credit." I would want them to take note and remember I did something for them. Sometimes I would even talk about our activities in front of my husband, Brian, as if to let *him* know I'd done something special with them. I was missing out on the joy of my children.

In the midst of the struggle, God was working in me. I was feeling low, but He caused me to look up. I wrote this in my journal:

> *I often feel like a failure, like I'm letting You and my kids down. I have even questioned Your wisdom in making me a mother.*
>
> *But You are sovereign, Lord. You are working out Your will. I know that this situation is not a surprise to you. Yes, there is more to this mothering thing than how I feel. <u>It isn't all about me</u>!*
>
> *Who am I to question You? Are You not God? To be praised and honored? Eternal? Higher than me?*

*Full of wisdom, knowledge and judgment beyond my
comprehension? Not in need of counsel? The One who made
and holds all things (my children and me included)? The
life-giver and healer? Over death and wounds? Firm in
Your grip upon me? Forever alive? You are Lord of and over
all, the sovereign King.*

*Who am I to question what You have done or what
You are doing? Forgive me, Lord. I see only me; You see
all of eternity. So this thing isn't about me. I am here and
You will change me. Oh, how I long to be more like You.*

As I read through my journal, I can see how God was preparing me for the work He wanted to do. I needed to be humbled. I was so full of myself, trying to do everything right and in my own strength. Did you notice that about me in the opening pages of this book? Have you ever been there? If I were to continue operating according to my own "wisdom" and best efforts, God would never be able to make me holy.

I needed to recognize who God is and submit to trusting Him. He is holy and perfect. His ways are higher than my ways, and His thoughts are higher than mine. He is my Creator and he holds all things together. He is not in need of counsel. He doesn't need my input to order my world. When I finally did acknowledge His sovereignty, trusting Him made perfect sense.

How about you? What is your view of God? Who do you say that He is? Do you believe His ways are perfect? Do you believe He is able to hold all of creation together in perfect balance? Do you believe He is big enough to handle your problems and order your world? If so, are you willing to submit to trusting Him?

## Someone to guide me

The time had come for me to have a mentor. Cathy called me and said she found someone who was willing to share her life with me. I was thrilled. I called Jenni and we set a time to meet. She was going to come over to my house for lunch and we would talk about when we could get together and what we would do.

The first day Jenni came over is still clear in my memory. I told the boys I had a friend coming over and they needed to give me alone time with her. My fear was they would overwhelm her and she'd never want to come back! I went around the living room and dining room vacuuming, dusting and straightening up. I wanted everything to look nice for Jenni. The thought, however, did cross my mind, "Is it bad to start this relationship out on a lie?" Soon enough, she would find out that my life wasn't neatly put together.

When Jenni walked through my front door, the first thing she did was hug me. Her warmth put me immediately at ease. I served her the lunch I had prepared and we talked about what it was going to be like to be in a mentoring relationship.

Jenni and I had a nice time together. True, the boys didn't give us anything that would count as "alone time," but we were able to talk, which was a good thing. I told Jenni about my desire to be holy and she suggested we read a book together. As God would have it, she knew just the book we should read. We chose **Growing Your Faith** by Jerry Bridges.

Before Jenni left, she told me about a retreat to which I was soon going to be receiving an invitation. It was a listening retreat she'd been to before and she was enthusiastic as she told me about it. The event sounded interesting to me — a time to be intentionally silent before God, listening for His voice. To be honest, though, at that time in my life almost anything to get me out of the house and away from my kids for 24 hours sounded interesting! I had no idea what God had in store for me.

## Getting ready

In the weeks preceding the retreat, I purchased a copy of **Growing Your Faith** and began reading. I was encouraged right away as I read the statement, "Nothing you ever do will cause [God] to love you anymore or any less. He loves you strictly by His grace given to you through Jesus."[1]

In theory, I was aware of that truth. In practice, however, I am a pleaser and somewhere inside of me I was afraid my failings as a mother disqualified me from some of God's love. When I didn't measure up to the perfect mommy standard, I secretly perceived I was less deserving of God's love. It seemed logical to me that when I lost my patience with my kids or when I selfishly withheld my attention from them, God would frown and withhold His love from me. I never expressed those thoughts, but it seemed reasonable to me that He would respond in such a way. Even as I write these words, I am ashamed I ever considered God could be so limited in His love.

What joy I experienced as I dwelt on the truth that my performance does not determine how much God loves me! That isn't to say I now felt I had the freedom to go out and do whatever I pleased and that my words and actions didn't matter, because God would still love me. On the contrary, my desire to please Him only increased. But now I held a confident assurance and joy, knowing He loved me; and that was one thing I couldn't mess up.

## Time to listen

Soon it was time to pack my bags, load up the van with a few new friends, and head up north for the "Listening in Christ" retreat. The retreat was being held at a Youth for Christ facility in northern Michigan. And, of course, it was raining when we arrived.

As we pulled into the parking lot, we were greeted with warm smiles and umbrellas. Jenni was there and she showed me to my room.

It was a nice retreat facility, but Jenni and the other women in charge had made it *lovely*. Each of us had a vase with a flower in it by our bed, including a note with a Bible verse, welcoming us to the retreat. Flowers, candles and chocolates were placed generously throughout the facility. Even the bathrooms had received their thoughtful touches.

After we were settled, we gathered together for our introduction to the retreat. Tricia, the retreat leader, talked to us about the process we were entering into, and our need to yield to God as we listen to Him. Before we dismissed, Tricia gave us our first listening assignment. In addition to thought-provoking questions to consider, we were instructed not to speak to anyone until breakfast time the next morning. So, in silent obedience, we went out to meet with God.

I returned to my room and found on my bed gifts from each of the two women who were praying for me while I was at the retreat. Each of them had carefully picked out and beautifully wrapped devotional books for me to use in my quiet times with God.

Also sitting on my bed was a love letter from God, and I was overwhelmed as I read it. The letter had some 55 scripture references in it and was written in the first person, as though God was speaking directly to me. My heart filled with joy as I considered that His thoughts toward me are as countless as the sand on the seashore (Psalm 139:17-18) and that He rejoices over me with singing (Zephaniah 3:17). I pondered the letter for a little while and then went out into the commons area to settle down and begin my assignment.

I sat there with my journal and a piece of paper which had this question on it, "What does Your loving heart want to say to me about who You are?"

For weeks I had been eagerly anticipating this event. I'd spent time each day praying about it and what God wanted to do, and I had two other women who were praying for me, too. At the time, though, I just sat wondering what to do next. I picked up my journal and began to write, somewhat matter-of-factly:

> *Here I am at the Listening in Christ retreat. Here I am to listen.*

As you continue with me on this journey, you're sure to discover music plays an important part in my life and song is one of the significant ways God speaks to me. At times, I find myself writing out the words of a song I know, as an outpouring of my heart. This is what happened as I continued to write in my journal that night.

> *"Here I am to worship. Here I am to bow down. Here I am to say that 'You're my God'. You're altogether lovely, altogether worthy, altogether wonderful to me. And I'll never know how much it cost to see my sin upon that cross. No, I'll never know how much it cost to see my sin upon that cross. So here I am to worship. Here I am to bow down. Here I am to say that 'You're my God!'"²*
>
> *You are worthy and lovely and wonderful. I worship You and bow down to only You and declare that You're my God. You took my sin upon Yourself at a price I'll never really understand.*
>
> *You are and deserve and have done all these things. You are high and exalted and worthy of praise. With my heart I will love and adore You. Worthy are You, Lord. All this, and <u>You</u> adore <u>me</u>? That thought seems too good to be true. But it <u>is</u> true, because Your word says so!*
>
> *Thank You for the gift of a love letter. You desire to lavish love upon me! Your love is everlasting! Your thoughts toward me are countless as the sand on the seashore! You rejoice over me with singing! You will never stop doing good to me!*
>
> *Such thoughts are almost too wonderful for me to grasp. I know that You are Mighty God, worthy of praise.*

*I want to know You and love You more. I know that
You love me – You gave up everything and even died for
me! You have opened up my eyes and spoken to me anew
of Your great love for me – that I am cherished. I am
Your treasured possession, Your beloved, yes, Your trophy.
Thank You, Lord, for loving me and for giving me a
glimpse of how great is Your love!*

*You simply love me. Nothing I do can increase or
decrease Your love for me. In some ways I wish that
weren't so. If I <u>do</u> the "right" things, won't Your love
increase? Can't I "earn" some bonus points? But that
way of thinking is so <u>me</u> — feeling the need to earn and
do. How gracious of You to not love me based upon my
performance. If I were able to "earn" Your love, then
surely I could (and probably would) lose it, too!*

*Lord, thank You that You never change. Thank You
that You are not fickle. Thank You that You operate on
will and decision, not on emotion.*

*So, here is the question of the night, "Lord, what does
Your loving heart want to say to me about who You are?"*

*You are the lover of my soul; the One who loves
me wholly, completely, perfectly, abundantly, purely,
eternally.*

*You are unchanging; steadfast in Your love; not swayed
or charmed, rather, constant.*

*You are faithful, providing for all that I need, never
leaving nor forsaking me.*

*You are high and exalted and worthy of praise. Holy
are You, Lord!*

That night, I was overwhelmed by the love of God. I had been a
believer for fourteen years and was confident God loved me. After
all, He went to the cross for me! Somehow, though, my understanding of His love had been limited.

I think I considered His love to be sacrificial, a Savior's love, love with a purpose. My sin had separated me from Him, and He didn't want for me to perish. So, out of love, He paid the price for my sin by dying in my place on the cross. Surely, that was proof of His love! "Greater love has no one than this, that he lay down his life for his friends."[3]

God gave me a greater view of His love, though. I read that His thoughts for me were countless as the sand on the seashore. He cherished me. He rejoiced over me with singing. My understanding grew so I realized He didn't just die to pay the price for my sins and save me from an eternity separated from Him. Rather, He died to pay the price for my sins *because He wanted to have a relationship with me for eternity.* Oh, my heart rejoices in this truth.

Do you know this love is for you, too? He is crazy about you. He thinks about you more often than there are grains of sand on the seashores. And that's a lot of sand! It doesn't matter what you've done or how much you've failed, or even how wonderful you think you are. He loves you because He loves you, and there's nothing you can do to change that fact. Won't you take a moment right now to sit and bask in that knowledge? Really. Put the book down and soak up God's incredible love for *you.*

## He loves me

The next morning at the Listening in Christ retreat, I found out the Love Letter from God which I had come to cherish over the night was more of a gift than I'd realized.

After breakfast, we sat and shared with each other what had happened the night before as we each met with God. When it was my turn to share, I talked about the Love Letter (of which I thought everyone had received a copy) and I read what I'd written in my journal. As the other women shared, and as I later confirmed with Jenni, I realized the Love Letter *wasn't* given to everyone. It was something God had put on Jenni's heart to give to me. How caring of Him! Of course His love is the same for all the women who were at the retreat, but He knew I needed to be covered in His love at that moment and He made it happen.

And so it was throughout the rest of the retreat — God lavished His love upon me. From the moments of silence in His presence, the walks and talks with new friends, the kind service of sisters in Christ who waited on us, and His tender attention of my heart, to the final moments of the retreat when our feet were washed and Tricia prayed for each of us individually, I was fully receiving His love.

When I got home, I could hardly tell my husband about the retreat because the tears of joy just wouldn't stop flowing. The next morning at church, when friends said, "Hi, Karen. How are you?" I just beamed and declared, "God loves me!" And when we began singing, God brought me back to Friday night as the band began to play, "Here I am to Worship." That song has become so precious to me, because each time I sing it, God takes me back again to the night when He declared His love for me so clearly.

## The work of the Spirit

God was leading me on a journey. He had put in my heart a desire to be holy, so I wanted to change. He had assured me that He is sovereign over all things, so I trusted Him. He had declared His love for me, so I felt secure. He was about to show me how He would bring it all to pass.

I mentioned before, my struggle was with "me." "I" seemed to get in the way of so many things, always wanting to do things; falsely thinking if it's going to be done right, I needed to do it. Part of the problem, I'm sure, was my pride and the other was that I'm impatient. I didn't want to wait for someone else to get the job done. I'd rather handle it myself; then at least I'd think progress was being made. What a fool I was!

### "No, Mommy. I do it myself!"

Let's pause here for just a moment so you can think about *your* tendencies. I'm guessing that, as a mother, you are all too familiar with the temptation to do the work yourself. Yes, the kids should clean up the mess they made, but you'll probably get it done better and faster if you do it yourself, right? Anyone could put the dishes away and wipe down the counter, but you know they probably won't, so you might as well take care of it. And the laundry? Well, clearly, it's *your* job, so do it! No one else will fold the towels just right anyway.

That line of thinking is often what goes through my head. But I have an excuse. *I was born this way.* Really! Just ask my mom. I've always been like this. My mom tells me my key phrase growing up was, "No, Mommy. I do it myself!"

At a very young age, I liked to dress myself. My mom would offer to help me, but I would look at her and say, "No, Mommy. I do it myself!" When we needed to go somewhere and I was taking too long putting on my shoes (Sorry, Mom!) she would plead with me, "Karen, will you please let me help you tie your shoes?" I looked at her and said, "No, Mommy. I do it myself!" When I graduated from high school, she had my cake decorated to include my favorite phrase. It said, "Mommy, I did it myself!"

Unfortunately, when we operate one way in the physical world, it is hard to operate a different way in the spiritual realm. If you are completely self-sufficient in your daily life, you probably tend to take that same attitude with you into your spiritual growth. At least that's what I find to be true in me. When I thought about growing spiritually, I spent a lot of time thinking about all the things *I* needed to do.

## "No, Karen. I'll do it Myself!"

If any progress was going to be made on my journey toward holiness, there *was* work to be done. And God, in His goodness, showed me that *I* wasn't the one who was going to be doing it!

I was continuing my study of **Growing Your Faith** when God revealed this understanding to me. The ongoing message in the book was that it is God's Spirit at work within us that will do the transforming.

> The Holy Spirit is the one responsible for this transformation. Paul said in 2 Corinthians 3:18 that we are being transformed by "the Lord, who is the Spirit." The verb *being transformed* is passive, that is, something is being done *to* us, not *by* us.
>
> This does not mean we have no responsibility in sanctification. It means that in the final analysis it is the Spirit of God who transforms us. He calls on us to cooperate synergistically and to do the part He assigns us to do, but He is the one who works deep within our character to change us.[4]

This idea was beginning to make sense to me — I have a role, but ultimately it is God who will transform me. Sometimes, however, God has to repeat Himself to me several times before something fully sinks into my heart. Though I'm not proud He has to do it, I love it when God repeats Himself, and this redundancy happened when He was teaching me about transformation by His Spirit.

One of the gifts I received at the Listening in Christ Retreat was a copy of Ruth Meyers' **31 Days of Praise**, and I was reading that book while I was going through **Growing Your Faith**.

On the same day Jerry Bridges was talking to me about the gospel as an instrument used by the Holy Spirit in our transformation, Ruth Meyers was leading me to praise God because He is transforming me into His image by His Spirit within me. I wrote in my journal:

> *You speak to me so clearly sometimes, even if it means repeating Yourself. Today I read in* **Growing Your Faith** *about the importance of the gospel in our transformation and the ongoing lesson has been that it is Your Spirit at work within us who will do the transforming. Now, in* **31 Days of Praise**, *I am led to praise You for Jesus – the life He lived and the example He is for me. And I am led to praise You because You transform me into His image by Your Spirit within me. Even 2 Corinthians 3:18 is repeated: You* are *transforming me into the likeness of Christ! Oh, how I long to be like Him, reflecting Him to the world around me!*

So, I was finally starting to "get it." God had put this desire in me to grow in holiness, and He was helping me understand that *He* would make it happen. In my way of seeing things, however, there was still a problem. Yes, I wanted to be holy, *but what about my kids?* How could I be both holy *and* a mother?

# Reflection Questions:

1. In what ways do you miss out on the joy of your children?

2. What might God need to do in you to prepare you to trust Him?

3. What prevents you from trusting God?

4. How does it make you feel that "nothing you ever do will cause God to love you any more or any less?"

5. What is your view of the Spirit's role in your transformation? Do you tend to be a do-it-yourself type, or is it easy for you to submit to Him?

6. What is keeping you from growing in holiness?

*≁ Chapter Four ≁*

# The Road to Holiness

As I read Growing Your Faith, I was simultaneously *en*couraged and *dis*couraged. Certainly realizing there is nothing I can do which will cause God to love me any more or any less, built my confidence. Likewise, I was eager to learn about growing more like Christ and encouraged that this book would help me in my pursuit of godliness. However, when I read the "twelve different positive character traits we should seek to put on: love, joy, peace, patience, kindness, goodness, faithfulness, gentleness, self-control, compassion, humility, and a forgiving spirit,"[1] I couldn't help but evaluate myself in my role as mother.

Hadn't I just yelled at someone for losing my "good" scissors? Didn't I just ignore another request to read that favorite book *again*? Wasn't I walking around with a sour look on my face and a grumpy spirit? Oh, the fruit of the spirit— love, joy, peace, patience, kindness, goodness, faithfulness, gentleness and self-control. I knew the list well, but those words did *not* describe me! Yet those traits were the things I was to "put on."

## Irritability and Impatience

Then I read about the things I was to "put off." In his discussion about the pursuit of holiness, Mr. Bridges said, "the basic meaning of holy is *separate*."[2] He said that just as God is separate from sin, He calls us to be separate from sin. Then he made *the list*. He wrote, "To pursue holiness is to take aggressive action to separate ourselves both from the sin within us: pride, selfishness, a critical and judgmental spirit, irritability, impatience, sexual lust, and so on..."[3] My heart stopped. Did I really read what I think I read? I looked again. Yes, there it was, in black and white: *irritability and impatience*.

I thought, "C'mon, I'm a mom! Wasn't I issued a license for irritability and impatience when I ordered my kids' birth certificates?" Let's think about this logically. First of all, these little darlings wreaked havoc on my body. Besides the enormous belly and throwing my hormones all out of whack, each one of my kids got on my nerves *before* they were even born! My sciatic nerve. That was painful.

Then they wouldn't let me sleep. Okay, Elizabeth slept through the night at 9 ½ weeks, but I spent the first three or four months of the boys' lives never sleeping more than four hours at a time! I remember one night when I complained about being tired and my husband didn't understand why. Hello! I hadn't gotten adequate sleep in four months!

Oh, let us not forget nursing. Before my first pregnancy, I was a size 36C. After nursing three babies, however, I shrank to a 34 *nearly* A. With each child, I had to get a new brassiere. (And I had thought I'd left padded cups behind in eighth grade!) Thanks a lot! Just *try* telling me I don't have the right to be *irritable*.

But we can't stop there. As they got older, they became more demanding. They learned to exert their wills, and that wonderful little word, "NO!" became a part of their vocabulary. As they got older still, they fought more with me and with each other, and "NO!"

turned into, "Not now," or, "Just a minute!" And the interruptions, oh, the interruptions…They never let me get anything done!

Take this morning, for example. I made arrangements several weeks ago for Elizabeth and Joshua to attend a camp at the Humane Society where they will get to learn about and spend time caring for animals. Today was the first day of their adventure. We went about our morning routine quickly, with our eye on the clock to get to camp on time.

As we were leaving, I noticed Elizabeth was wearing her flip-flops which I wasn't so crazy about, but I figured, "Why fight her on this one. She likes wearing them…Whatever." Of course, I would come to regret that thought later.

When we pulled into the parking lot of the Humane Society, I picked up the directions to find out which door we were to use. It was then I saw the "Attire" section of the information letter which read, "Shoes should cover the entire foot (no sandals)."

I was pretty sure flip-flops fell into that category and realized I needed to go home and get Elizabeth her tennis shoes. Ugh! Why didn't I read this letter more carefully before? Why didn't I just insist Elizabeth wear tennis shoes in the first place? But I didn't, and I had to take care of the problem now. It was an inconvenience, but not such a big deal. I could get home and be back with her shoes in about 25 minutes. So I said, "Goodbye," and Matthew and I set off to gather appropriate footwear.

Just as we were pulling out of the parking lot, Matthew *yelled* that he was thirsty. How this thirst came upon him so quickly, and why he couldn't have asked for a drink 60 seconds earlier when we were in a building with a drinking fountain, I don't know. I'll admit to lacking compassion when I told him he'd need to wait until we got home. It would be less than 15 minutes, and I knew he wasn't going to shrivel up before his desire could be satiated. So I drove on, doing my best to block out his whining.

When we got home I ran into the house to get the shoes and a drink. Matthew followed me in, having just realized he was also about to die of starvation, begging and pleading with me for a snack. I went into the pantry in the basement and grabbed something for him, then rushed him back into the van.

We made it all the way to the end of our street and were waiting at the stoplight when Matthew's next emergency arose. He had to use the bathroom. *Now*. Fortunately, we were right next to a gas station so I pulled into the parking lot and the attendant allowed Matthew to use the facilities.

Back in the van, we had traveled less than half a mile when I turned the corner and saw a train crossing the street. "Oh well," I thought. "This will only take a minute."

While we were waiting for the train, Matthew had another emergency bathroom need. I tried to convince him he was able to wait until we got to the Humane Society. I wondered aloud why he didn't take care of all of his needs at the gas station. I begged him to "hold it" for just 10 more minutes. Then I decided I didn't want that kind of mess in the van, so in desperation I pulled into the parking lot of a tavern in front of which we were standing. It was only 10:30 in the morning and this establishment didn't serve breakfast, but they were open! Thank You, Jesus!

I stood outside of the bathroom labeled "Bucks," (the other one was for "Does" – I figured, although Matthew isn't quite a Buck, he definitely isn't a Doe...) tapping my foot wishing Matthew would hurry up and come out. Then I remembered I told him to make sure he took care of *everything* this time. Oh, yeah. So I waited.

When he finally came out and we got in the van to deliver the tennis shoes to the Humane Society, I realized this little inconvenience wasn't going to set me back a mere 25 minutes. All totaled, the ordeal took more than an hour.

You know, I could have used that hour to make my menu and grocery list, and fold a couple loads of laundry. Instead, I was running around getting things for my kids, listening to whining and waiting for, well, nature. Go ahead; tell me I have no grounds to be *impatient*. It makes sense to me!

## It isn't *my* fault

Please tell me this line of thinking makes sense to you. I may be irritable and impatient, but I'm not irrational, am I? For all the things our kids "put us through," isn't it perfectly logical that we should walk around upset and irritable most of the time? What creature in her right mind would smile at nights of missed sleep, days of endless whining and complaining, and years of flab where there used to be a firm tummy? I am making sense, am I not?

Oh, I can rationalize with the best of them, but the truth is, I felt so negative most of the time. And I didn't like it one bit. While it is true I thought I was justified in my sour disposition, feeling justified didn't make me *feel* any better. Now, I won't pretend to know the mind of God, but I am confident that being an irritable, impatient, grumpy, dissatisfied mother was *not* His goal for me. Are you seeing yourself at all here?

So, I had this desire building inside of me. I *wanted* to be a reflection of Him. I understood there were things I needed to "put on," and there was sin from which I needed to separate myself. God had made it clear that He would do the work. I *really* wanted to change, but (get ready for a glimpse at my awesome maturity) I felt like my kids kept ruining it! They had a way. They knew how to push my buttons. They could get me so angry. How could I reconcile what I really *wanted* with what was *real*? That's when God opened my eyes.

## Adversity with a purpose

I was reading the chapter in **Growing Your Faith** called "Trusting God." That particular chapter talks about adversity, and how God uses the hard times in our lives. While it may seem a bit harsh, I felt I could put my children and my mothering struggles in the category of "adversity." That's just where I was.

In his discussion, Mr. Bridges said, "[God] knows exactly what and how much adversity will develop more Christ-likeness in us, and He will not bring, nor allow to come into our lives, any more than is needful for His purpose."[4]

Honestly, I wanted to argue with him. While I agree God is all-knowing, I just couldn't see how this adversity in my life was "needful." To me, it seemed like my struggles with my children were preventing me from becoming the godly woman I so wanted to be.

Perhaps you too have been at this place. Have you ever had in mind what you would like to have happen, like becoming a godly woman, and you think, "If only this or that were different, I could be that person." Or what about the line, "Well, if you would just obey me, I wouldn't yell so much!" I will admit to having said something like that once or twice. With that frame of mind, it was hard for me to see how the struggles I have with my children could possibly be "needful."

In the midst of my private argument, Mr. Bridges broke through with the statement that unlocked the door to my understanding. He wrote, "The road to holiness is *paved with adversity*."[5] [emphasis mine]

Oh! What a wonderful revelation! It wasn't my children who were going to keep me from drawing nearer to God and becoming holy. Rather, it was my children that God was going to use to take me there! That was my "aha!" moment, when I began to understand *God is using my children to make me into the woman that He wants me to be.*

This discovery took me back to a moment that had occurred months before. I was worn and weary, ready to give up after another episode with one of my children. Though I don't remember for certain, I'm guessing I was in tears as I was lamenting my struggles to my husband. Brian thought for a moment and then said, "Maybe God is using them as part of your sanctification."

At the time I wanted to hit him. How could he be so insensitive? But here I was, hearing the same message again. (Remember what I said about God repeating Himself to me?) Now I wanted to hug Brian and tell him how wise he is! My hope was increasing even more as I thought about God using my children to transform me.

## Making it clear

God confirmed this idea of transformation for me, shortly after I discovered it. My daughter was with my parents, my husband was away at a conference for work, and my mother-in-law wanted the boys. That left me, all by myself! From Monday night until Thursday afternoon, I had nobody to whom I needed to answer. I left the house when I wanted to, and came home when I felt like it. It didn't matter when or what I prepared for breakfast, lunch or dinner — or even if I prepared anything at all! Nobody cared when I went to bed at night or what time I got up in the morning. I was *free*! (Please note that my intention in sharing this with you is to illustrate a lesson, not to fill you with coveting and jealously!)

I had a friend who had wanted me to come over and sit in her hot tub with her sometime. So I called her up and made plans. It was about seven o'clock in the evening when I arrived at her house. (Maybe grandma was thinking about bath time, but I wasn't!) We slipped into the hot tub and talked and laughed and enjoyed time relaxing. When we decided we "ought" to get out, we were surprised to find that it was 11:15! Where had the time gone? Who cared?

Being the responsible adults we are, we decided we should call it a night…after a mug of hot chocolate. An hour later, I finally said good-bye to my friend and went home. Who knew? Who cared? I found out later that my neighbors did. My un-married, care-free, live-for-the-moment neighbors were concerned, wondering where the kids were and why I was out so late. They're so sweet!

I thoroughly enjoyed my "time off." Before I had children, I had no idea it was possible to *crave* time alone. Now, as a mother, I relish the times when no one is asking me to do something, get something or go somewhere. I even consider it a treat to be able to run errands for my husband if I get to do it alone.

The time off I had was a gift given to me by God and also an avenue He used to assure me that the road to holiness *is* paved with adversity. You see, by Thursday morning, I was feeling pretty good about myself. I wasn't irritable *or* impatient. I hadn't yelled at anyone for days. I thought, "Change? Who needs to change? I'm perfect!"

Of course I *seemed* perfect. No one was around making demands of me or leaving messes for me to clean up. I was never faced with the choice of doing what *I* wanted to do or what *someone else* wanted me to do. There were no fights for me to settle, broken toys for me to fix, or scraped knees to interrupt my plans for the day. Under those circumstances, who *wouldn't* seem perfect?

So it was clear. God *is* using my children to transform me. I *need* them so that, by the work of God's Spirit, I can conquer my irritability and impatience (among other things) and begin to be a reflection of Him.

## Reflection Questions:

1. What makes you irritable and impatient?

2. Do you feel like your kids are keeping you from becoming more Christ-like?

3. What else is "keeping" you from growing?

4. How do you think God might be using that very thing to accomplish His purpose in you?

~ *Chapter Five* ~

# For The Bible Tells Me So

**Do you remember** the song "Jesus Loves Me?" Perhaps you grew up singing it. Maybe you have children who sing it. The words are quite simple, but speak volumes of truth. "Jesus loves me, this I know. For the Bible tells me so...Yes, Jesus loves me. The Bible tells me so."[1]

That little song helps us learn of God's love for us. I thought I could change it a bit to help me learn a new lesson. How's this? "Jesus transforms me this I know. For the Bible tells me so...Yes, Jesus transforms me. The Bible tells me so." Hmmm...maybe not. But the Bible *does* tell me so!

## Paul said - "Rejoice in our sufferings"

When I was beginning to understand God was using the hard times in my life to transform me, I was amazed at how many times I came across that same idea in the Bible. I was in a Precept Ministries Bible study, led by my mentor, Jenni. We were studying the book of Romans when I saw it.

Romans 5:2 says, "We rejoice in the hope of the glory of God." That sounds reasonable. Verse 3 goes on to say, "Not only so, but we also rejoice in our sufferings…" What? Why would we rejoice in *that*? Keep reading! "…because we know that suffering produces perseverance; perseverance, character; and character, hope."

Off the topic for just a moment, Precept Ministries, which was founded by Kay Arthur and her husband, Jack, teaches inductive Bible study. Participants are taught how to study the Bible precept upon precept and, as such, are encouraged not to resort to commentaries for quick and easy answers. Every now and then, however, at the end of a lesson, Kay would "give us permission" to consult commentaries to supplement the things we had learned.

It was at one of these times when we were allowed to look at commentaries that I gained valuable insight into Romans 5:2-4. I read in **Romans**, by John Stott, the word "character" in verse 3 referred to "the quality of a person who has been tested and has passed the test."[2] *And has passed the test*. I liked that.

I thought, "Yes. I would like to have that quality." But as Stott pointed out in the passage, the quality comes from *perseverance*, and without *suffering* there would be nothing through which we need to persevere. Therefore, if I'm going to have such a character quality, I'm going to need to go through trials. So, we rejoice in our suffering!

## James said - "Trials are pure joy"

On another day when I was pondering this idea, God brought to my mind another familiar passage about trials. James 1:2-3 says, "Consider it pure joy, my brothers, whenever you face trials of many kinds." Pure joy? That sounds like something *really* good. Like, better than a king size Reese's Peanut Butter cup with no one around with whom you have to share it!

Did he really mean "pure joy?" And what about "whenever?" That sounds like something which is going to happen more than once — maybe even lots of times!

One more question: He said trials of "many kinds." Uh, that definitely sounds like something is going to happen more than once. How could it possibly elicit pure joy?

I guess we need to keep reading. James 1:3-4 says, "because you know the testing of your faith develops perseverance. Perseverance must finish its work so that you may be mature and complete, not lacking anything."

There it was again! Trials develop perseverance, which results in maturity. See what I mean about God repeating Himself? I love that He is so patient and persistent with me.

I am very familiar with this passage from James. It is one of the first Bible verses I memorized many years ago. I have heard it quoted often in sermons and have read various authors' thoughts about it, too.

For some reason, though, it took a long time for me to "get it." I spent years quoting, "Consider it pure joy, my brothers…" without realizing what pure joy is and that it could really come as a result of trials. Admittedly, I simply read the words and let them slip through my mind without trying to make sense of them.

In God's timing, and by His grace, I had finally come to understand this truth. The trials in my life and yours will produce perseverance in us. And when perseverance finishes its work, what joy! I don't know about you, but I think I could muster up some pure joy, knowing that I am mature and complete, not lacking anything!

## The psalmist said - "Testing refines us"

Some weeks later, He drove it home one more time. I was reading Ruth Meyers' **The Satisfied Heart: 31 Days of Experiencing God's Love** and continued to come across instances of God using trials to mature us and show us His love. On Day 11, He showed me something wonderful.

Ruth was sharing about a time when God had spoken to her about how He uses difficult circumstances in our lives as she studied Psalm 66:10-12.

> "For You, O God, tested us;
> You refined us like silver.
> You brought us into prison and laid burdens
> on our backs.
> You let men ride over our heads;
> We went through fire and water;
> But You brought us to a place of abundance."

She wrote, "Through this passage the Lord reminded me of how He works: He uses not only discouragement but also desperate situations to bring new release and enlargement into our lives — greater fulfillment and abundance and growth. The more desperate and impossible our situation, the more glory it can bring to God."[3]

I was in agreement with what she said and was thankful for yet another example of how God uses trials in our lives for good. However, the part of this passage that *really* stood out to me was verse 10, "For You, O God, tested us; You refined us like silver."

I responded to God's word to me in my journal:

> *O, my God, You are so good! And I am so thankful.*
> *I am amazed that You keep showing me that You use tri-*
> *als to refine us. Over and over. You are making Yourself*
> *clear and I love it.*
>
> *I am especially taken with this image of being refined*
> *like silver. I remember the description I once heard of how*
> *silver is refined — that it is put in very hot fire and the*
> *impurities are burned out, until the silversmith sees his*
> *reflection.*
>
> *It brings me such joy to know that You love me and*
> *want to transform me into a holy woman! And so, Lord,*
> *I welcome the trials because I want to be like You. I want*
> *to be holy just like You. I want the impurities to be*
> *burned out of me so that when You look at me, You will*
> *see Your reflection so clearly!*

The first image of transformation I received which really made sense to me was that of the road to holiness which was paved with adversity. Now a second image — that of silver being refined — brought me even greater joy. With the first image, I was able to better understand the *reason* for the trials. The second image gave me greater hope for the *destination.* Oh, to be like Jesus!

## Ready for refining

And so I came to the end of the preparation stage. God, in His own way, had sorted, washed, and sifted me. He had started re-moving some of the big "chunks" that were keeping me from being like Him. In His wisdom and goodness, He had convinced me of His love and led me to trust Him. The gentleness with which He handled me assured me I was going to be okay. Having gone through the time of preparation, I was ready to move on to the refining process.

Just as I am convinced God is interested in the silver resting in your soul, I also believe He will prepare you for the work He wants to do in you. His ways are perfect and He knows exactly what you need. He will deal with you gently and lovingly, desiring to win your trust. It is my sincere hope that you will recognize His good and loving hand at work in your life, and that you will choose to trust Him as He works to transform you.

# Reflection Questions:

1. Do you believe you can rejoice in your suffering?

2. How can you view your trials as pure joy?

3. How does it make you feel that God is testing you?

4. How do these two images — of the road to holiness which is paved with adversity and silver which is being refined — help you think about the process of becoming holy?

## PART III

# The Refining

*"A fierce fire is always necessary in refining silver."*[1]

When the ore from the silver mines had gone through the process of preparation and smelting, it was ready to be refined. The refiner would place the cakes of silver on a grate and heat them up in order that they may be more easily broken. After breaking the silver into chunks, he carefully placed it into the furnace to begin the refining process.[2]

It took about an hour for the silver chunks to melt and another two to three hours for the refining process to be completed, depending on whether the silver was pure or impure to begin.[3] During this time of refining, the extreme heat of the fire caused the impurities within the silver to surface and burn away.

According to a popular story about refining silver, the silversmith was able to tell when the purification process was completed because he would be able to see his reflection in the molten silver.[4]

~ *Chapter Six* ~

# Living Through the Fire

IT WAS GOING TO BE "one of those nights." I knew what to expect because I'd been through it so many times before, but I wanted it to be different this time. Brian was going to be gone at bedtime, and it was a bath night. Going solo for bedtime is never fun and when it includes a bath night, well, let's just say it usually isn't pretty.

Nonetheless, I had it as my goal to keep my cool with the kids on this particular night. I knew God was using my children to transform me, and I wanted them to see that work in progress. My hope was for a peaceful, enjoyable bedtime, with laughter and lots of hugs and kisses. I didn't want to raise my voice at the kids, much less yell at them about anything.

I envisioned children coming inside when I called them, happily cleaning up their toys at the first prompting, proceeding immediately to the shower when their toys were neatly stored, and accomplishing all of these tasks without complaining or arguing. Admittedly, my head may have been in the clouds, but my heart was yearning to reflect the love of God to my children. And, if the evening went that smoothly, then surely I could be the gentle, loving mother I longed to be.

So, what really happened? Well, they didn't come in when I called them. Clean up (as much of it as was actually completed) was not done happily, nor was it done after only one prompting. Fights broke out over who got to use the bathroom upstairs and who had to shower downstairs, while I was trying to convince them I couldn't possibly be upstairs with one and stay downstairs with another at the same time. The evening's tasks were definitely not accomplished without complaining or arguing, and I didn't make it through without raising my voice. In fact, I yelled at them a time or two...or three.

After I'd tucked the boys in, I went to Elizabeth's room to say goodnight to her. I was on the verge of tears, disappointed with the way I'd handled myself in the midst of the chaos, but I figured if I could just say a quick goodnight and excuse myself, I'd be okay. But a prompt exit wasn't going to happen either.

Elizabeth asked me to sing to her. (For me, singing to the kids is a standard bedtime practice, but somehow I'd managed to slip out of the boys' room without being asked to sing.) I took a deep breath and started in on "Somewhere Over the Rainbow," which is Elizabeth's usual request. It didn't take long before I felt the tears coming and I excused myself to the bathroom to try to regain my composure, promising I'd be back in just a minute. I don't know why this happens to me, but if I'm feeling emotional, I simply cannot sing without crying. And so it went that night.

When I was ready, I went back into Elizabeth's room to give it another try. However, instead of hearing the song, she wanted to know why I was crying. I tried to explain, "Honey, I want to reflect Jesus to you and your brothers. I want to be kind and loving to you all the time. Instead of getting frustrated and upset, I want to have patience and stay calm. So, when I get angry and start yelling like I did tonight, it makes me sad because I know that I'm not reflecting Jesus to you. That's why I was crying, because I'm sad about the way I was acting."

Her reply was priceless. She said, "Mommy, do you know what I do when that happens to me? I pray. Let's pray right now." So we did. It was beautiful. My nine year old little girl brought me before the throne of God and ministered hope to me.

As you are in the trenches of motherhood, I do hope you will see the ways in which He uses your little ones to pour His love into you.

## Prayer – a lifeline

Are you familiar with the show *"Who Wants To Be A Millionaire?"* Each contestant receives three lifelines on their quest to acquire a million dollars. As each question gets progressively more difficult, they have the option of polling the audience, eliminating two of the multiple choice answers, or phoning a friend.

Prayer has become a vital lifeline for me as I seek to live through the refining fire. Talking to God before proceeding with my decisions gives me the assurance I'm on the right path. And, unlike the contestants on the game show, I have unlimited access to God.

I have a habit of getting up in the morning before the rest of the family so that I can have quiet time to pray and read my Bible. I cherish those quiet moments.

I believe it is important to have planned times of prayer when we get "away" — whether it's in a remote location or just behind a closed door — and focus our attention on God. We need to make time to communicate with God and allow him to speak to us. Jesus went away to solitary places to be with His Father. Certainly, we need to as well.

I do not in any way want to downplay this kind of communion with God, but honestly, most of my praying happens when it is anything but quiet around me. I have become increasingly aware of God's abiding presence within me and have begun to answer Paul's call to "pray continually." It has become clear to me that I cannot "do" this mothering thing on my own, rather, I *must* call upon God to lead me through. So I talk to Him all the time, and I know He is listening.

Jan Johnson has led a couple of women's retreats which I have attended at my church and she has given me helpful insights into this practice of praying continually. Jan shared with us the idea of "breath prayers." Simply put, breath prayers are short phrases you can say, literally, in a breath.

Jan said one of her favorite breath prayers is, "Show me his heart." I have used that one often, in seeking to understand my children. Another of my frequent breath prayers is, "Help me to love them." When my children are driving me crazy I close my eyes, take a deep breath, and as I exhale I pray, "Help me to love them."

On my own, I fail. I *need* God to love my children through me.

I remember one night, though there have been several just like it, when I felt like I was literally having a constant conversation with God. It was a Friday night, which means "movie night" at our house.

Every Friday, one of the kids gets to select a movie from the video store to watch after we've eaten dinner, cleaned up the house, and put on pajamas. We usually settle down and watch the movie together, eating popcorn and enjoying one another's company. Enjoy, that is, until one of the kids — or sometimes Mom — realizes how tired they are.

On this particular night, I think someone was tired before the movie even started. It seemed nothing was going right. One child wanted to start the movie right away. Another wanted to wait to see if our neighbors could come over. The other one didn't want them to come at all because sometimes they run around and make too much noise during the movie. I was begging God to give me patience amidst all the arguing.

When we finally began the movie, the kids started in with the requests. "Will you get us popcorn?" "Can I have a drink?" "Sit here!" "Do we have any candy?" "Will you get my blanket?" "Mom, when are you going to watch the movie?" "Can I have more popcorn?" God has shown me before He loves to meet my needs and reminded me of that fact on movie night as my children were making their requests known. So, as I made my way through the night, I was doing my own asking; I prayed that God would give me joy in meeting my children's needs even as He loves to meet mine.

Shortly after the movie was over, the bottom fell out. Joshua was tired and needed to go to bed, but didn't want to go upstairs alone. And when he is *that* tired, look out! The problem was, neither Elizabeth nor Matthew wanted to go to bed yet, and Brian and I both had things to attend to downstairs. However, we assured him one of us would go upstairs "soon."

Meanwhile, Joshua was yelling about wanting "everyone" to go to bed so he wasn't upstairs by himself. Elizabeth was yelling at Joshua for yelling and Matthew was just running around yelling for no particular reason, except he didn't want to be left out of all the commotion.

As I was getting ready to go upstairs, trying not to give in to the chaos around me, I was praying again. I prayed, "He's tired, Lord. Please help me to remember that. He's tired, Lord. Please help me to love him. He's tired, Lord. Please give me grace to give to him." We did make it through the night and everyone was in much better spirits the next day.

If you aren't already, I encourage you to explore this practice of praying continually. God is ever present and wanting to help you. Think of all the times when your children are struggling to do something and you watch them thinking, "If you would just ask me, I would help you!" God is *always* watching you, and *always* willing to help you. Just ask Him!

## The Word

God's Word has been another important key for me in living through the refining fire. Having been encouraged by some wonderful, godly people to do it, I decided I wanted to make a regular practice of memorizing scripture.

Some people suggest writing out verses and taping them on your mirror, in the cupboards, in the car, and various other places you are regularly looking. They say by having the verse hanging there, you'll see it often and be able to commit it to memory. Sounds reasonable.

For some reason, I frequently put my hands in my pockets and when I noticed this habit one day, I decided to take a different approach to memorization. Rather than hanging verses, I decided to fold them up and put them in my pocket. Then, whenever I put my hand in my pocket, I would feel the paper, take it out, and read it. So this is what I did, and it worked well.

God took this exercise a step further, though, from just memorizing verses to shaping my character and speaking His love to me.

It had become a habit of mine, in the middle of my mothering struggles, to ask, "God, what is it You want to work in me right now?" Quite often, in response to that question I would get a sense God was giving me opportunities to practice being patient, or gentle, or kind.

So when I felt Him prompting me in such a way, I would look for a Bible verse dealing with that character trait, write it down, and stick it in my pocket. Then, throughout the day, I would feel the piece of paper and read the verse, and be reminded of the ways God wanted to work in me.

For instance, it has happened this way before: It's a Monday, which is my day to do laundry, go grocery shopping, and volunteer in Matthew's classroom. Matthew is in afternoon kindergarten so I get some of the laundry done in the morning before I take him to school. After I drop him off, I go shopping, put the groceries away at home, and drive up to school to volunteer.

My children's school is very big on parental involvement and as long as my kids still think it's "cool" for Mom to be in their classroom, I'm going to be there!

When school is over we pile into the van and head for home. The kids are anxious to tell me about their day and everyone is talking at once. At home there is a rush to get snacks and turn on the TV or play a game on the computer when I ask the question, "What about your homework?"

The atmosphere instantly changes from fun to fighting because no one wants to do homework, and I need to get back to housework. As I try to reason with them, I can feel myself getting tense, but I feel something else, too. It's that paper in my pocket and I take it out to read, "Be completely humble and gentle; be patient, bearing with one another in love." (Ephesians 4:2) And I thank God for reminding me to be gentle and patient with my children.

At other times I came across verses, whether in my own reading or by hearing someone else share them, that I thought would carry me through some of the hard times I face each day. So I began to write them down and carry them around in my pocket.

A speaker at a conference I attended shared one such verse, "Though you pass through the waters, I will be with you; and when you pass through the rivers, they will not sweep over you. When you walk through the fire you will not be burned; the flames will not set you ablaze." (Isaiah 43:2)

How often with my children do I feel like I'm going to be swept over by the waters or consumed by the fire? But I hold on to promises like this one from Isaiah and thank God for protecting me.

This practice of carrying scripture in my pocket has been a delight to me. Sometimes I put on a pair of pants that I haven't worn in a while and when I put my hand in the pocket, I find a verse I'd forgotten to take out. I always read it with a smile, like it's a love note God planted for me.

Other times, if I *know* I'm going to face particular challenges on a certain day, I will select an appropriate Bible verse and carry it with me. "Let the peace of Christ rule in your hearts," (Colossians 3:15) is a favorite of mine. You know what the Boy Scouts say, "Be Prepared!"

*For more thoughts about carrying scripture in your pocket, see Appendix A.*

## Just sing, sing a song

Ever since I was a little girl I have loved singing, and song is another vehicle God uses to carry me through the refining fire. You've heard the adage, "Music tames the savage beast." That saying is absolutely true for me. I don't know what makes it so but, if I am having a hard time, singing lifts my soul. My children know what to do when I say, "Mommy just needs to sing right now." They step back and understand that, in a few minutes, I'll be nice again.

Several years ago, Kathy Troccoli and Sandy Patti recorded an album of classic popular songs which included "Somewhere Over the Rainbow." Something about singing that song with them at the top of my lungs can get me past the foulest of moods and over the biggest disappointments.

I remember one day when I sang it probably three or four times before I turned and realized the window was open and my husband was outside talking with our neighbors. That night I asked him if they'd heard my "therapy session." He assured me they had not. I never pressed him to find out if he was telling the truth or if he was just being nice, but I do check the windows now.

On another occasion, I was in the kitchen after an episode with one of my kids. I was feeling upset with myself for getting angry and yelling over an inconsequential event. It was so unimportant that now I can't even remember what it was about. What I do remember is that I was feeling terrible.

God had entrusted three precious children to my care. He was giving me opportunities to grow in Christ-likeness and here I was blowing my top over petty issues. I needed to sing and turned on Kathy Trocolli's "Stubborn Love."

*Caught again*
*Your faithless friend*
*Don't You ever tire of hearing what a fool I've been*
*Guess I should pray*
*What can I say*
*Oh, it hurts to know the hundred times I've caused*
*You pain*
*The "forgive me" sounds so empty when I never change*
*Yet You stay and say You love me*
*Still forgiving me time and time again*

*It's Your stubborn love*
*That never lets go of me*
*I don't understand how You can stay*
*Perfect love embracing the worst in me*
*How I long for Your stubborn love*

*Funny me*
*Just couldn't see*
*Even long before I knew You, You were loving me*
*Sometimes I cry*
*You must cry too*
*When You see the broken promises I've made to You*

*I keep saying that I'll trust You tho' I seldom do*
*Yet You stay and say You love me still*
*Knowing someday I'll be like You*

*It's Your stubborn love*
*That never lets go of me*
*I don't understand how You can stay*
*Perfect love embracing the worst in me*
*How I long for Your stubborn love*[1]

I had sung this song countless times before, but somehow on that day it was as if I heard the line, "Knowing someday I'll be like You," for the very first time. As the words rolled off my tongue and registered in my heart, the tears started pouring from my eyes.

Just moments before, I had been yelling at one of my kids for something. (I don't even remember who was the victim of my tirade.) I was feeling like I was letting God down in every possible way, and now I sensed He was telling me there was still hope for me. Some day I *will* be like Him. Talk about stubborn love!

Needless to say, after that "therapy session" not only were my spirits lifted, but my soul was encouraged. And another title was added to my personal list of "Songs that take me back to significant moments with God."

## Imagine

I have learned one other practice that helps me to live while I'm in the refining fire. The small group Bible study of which I am a part was talking one night about our individual desires to grow more Christ-like. We decided to take a goal setting exercise my husband had learned and apply it our spiritual growth.

Our assignment was to write out our spiritual goals and report back to the group the next week. An important part of writing out these goals is you write them *as if they've already happened*. You get to imagine God's work in you is already completed.

I found this exercise to be absolutely wonderful. Thinking about what I want to "look like," and writing it down as if it were a done deal was so encouraging! An especially helpful aspect of this assignment was we were supposed to write out the goals every day. There's something about repetition that really works for me.

Do you remember what I said about the words love, joy, peace, patience, kindness, goodness, faithfulness, gentleness, and self-control *not* describing me? Well, as I thought about what I want to look like, those words came back to me. This is what I came up with:

*I am being refined by a holy God, transformed into a holy woman. This transformation bears fruit in the following ways:*

*1. I am filled to overflowing with the love of Christ.*

*2. I have abundant joy — when I am doing what I want and when I am bowing to the desires of others.*

*3. I am peaceful, remaining calm even when under pressure and being pulled in many directions.*

*4. I am patient, able to wait calmly rather than resorting to yelling, nagging, or counting.*

*5. I am kind. I go out of my way to say and do nice things to everyone - especially my family.*

*6. I am good. I make decisions and behave in ways that are pleasing and honoring to God.*

*7. I am faithful. What I say, I will do and people know that they can count on me.*

8. *I am gentle. When someone is hurting, I can make them feel better. Even in disciplining my children I am careful not to harm them physically, spiritually, or emotionally.*

9. *I am self-controlled. By the grace of God, I do not fly off the handle in a rage when provoked.*

*This transformation is also evidenced in these ways:*

1. *I am constantly aware of God's abiding presence within me.*

2. *I am sensitive to God's voice and He speaks to me often.*

3. *I am obedient to God's call, so He often prompts me to pray for people and situations.*

4. *I am increasingly aware of my inability to do anything good or worthwhile on my own, and I give thanks to God for the work He does in and through me by the power of His Spirit.*

5. *I am the same person at home with my children as I am on stage speaking to women and on paper writing my story.*

6. *I am an instrument that God is using for His glory. When women hear me speak, they see God in me — His reflection — and they are drawn to Him.*

I began to live as though those things were true about me. One day Matthew asked me to play a game with him. Honestly, I didn't want to play it but agreed to anyway, though my attitude was begrudging. Then I thought, "I have abundant joy — when I am doing what I want to do and when I am bowing to the desires of others." And I *chose* to be joyful as we played together.

I am in the fire. No question about that. By God's grace, I have learned that I can *live* in the fire. I reach out to Him and He carries me — through prayer, His word, song, and a picture of possibility. He never gives us more than we can bear. Remember, *He* is the One doing the work here! I love that He has shown me the ways He will help me live.

The same is true for you. Though you may be in the refining fire right now, you can live. I know you can pray. And you can hide God's word in your heart. (Or in your pocket, as the case may be!) Maybe singing isn't really your idea of a good time, but I know there is *something* you can do to lift your spirits when times are hard.

So, what is it that lifts you up? Some women enjoy crafts, or reading, or taking a walk. I have one friend who tells me when she's feeling confused or frustrated, going for a long run is all she needs to clear her mind and get her back on track. (I will *never* understand how that helps!)

Perhaps you could also try writing out your own spiritual goals. Though you're in the middle of the fire, you can think about what the end will be. Go ahead and dream big! When my husband first heard me read, "I am peaceful, remaining calm even when under pressure and being pulled in many directions," he looked at me like I was crazy. I smiled and reminded him these were *goals*.

Certainly, the ideas I have suggested are not the *only* things you can do to live in the fire. God may very well lay other things on your heart. He knows you much better than I do! I aim only to share with you the ways in which God has led me in order to give you encouragement.

## Reflection Questions:

1. How can you incorporate prayer and God's Word into every moment of your life?

2. Will you consider writing out your spiritual goals? Write them each day for at least a week. Allow God to mold them and you in the process. Dream big!

3. What else can help you live in the fire?

## Chapter Seven

# Growing in the Fire

SOMETIMES I WONDER WHERE I AM in this refining process. If it took one hour for the silver to melt, and another two to three for the refining to be completed, how far along am I? Have I even started melting yet? Not that I want to die soon, for I know that I won't be perfect this side of heaven, but sometimes I wonder if I'm making any progress.

## Discontentment with sin

I have heard it said that as you grow closer to God, you become more discontent with the sin in your life. Some people have likened it to a mess in a dark room. When the light isn't on, the room doesn't seem so bad. Flip the switch, though, and the messy condition becomes a problem that needs addressing. The light reveals the true condition of the room.

So it is with God and us. The more we draw near to Him, the more His light shines into the dark corners of our heart, the more we see our messy condition. Yet, the fear of seeing the "mess" in our hearts should not keep us from seeking Him. Please don't let me discourage you from drawing near to God! Because in Jesus Christ, He has made a way for us to be clean.

I have witnessed this play out in my own life. As I was becoming more and more convinced that God was transforming me through the struggles I have as a mother, my confidence and joy in Him was growing. My desire to draw near to Him was increasing, and I poured out my heart to Him in my journal. I wrote:

> *I praise You for Your goodness. You are eternal, unchanging. Your love is unending. Your faithfulness endures forever. You are holy, perfect in all Your ways. You are the Just Judge, Sovereign Lord, Creator of heaven and earth. All these things are true of You and still You care for me. And so I give You my life – it is Yours – I surrender.*
>
> *So I lay before You my sin. Irritability. Pride. Self-centeredness. I have been so negative. I have been unkind. I have snapped. I have been complaining. I have been selfish. And that's just today!*
>
> *What a wretched wreck I am. Lord, forgive me. Thank You for Your precious blood to cleanse me from all unrighteousness, to free me from the bondage of sin.*
>
> *Your love is great. My hope is in You!*

The more I became aware of how holy God is, the more I became aware of how far I fall short of Him. All the while God was revealing my sin to me, though, my desire to grow and be more like Him was increasing. I just wanted *more* of Him.

## Aggravation

We had finished dinner, the dishes were washed, homework was completed, and there was still about half an hour before the kids needed to get ready for bed. One might think that string of accomplishments would be cause for rejoicing, and on some nights it might be, but on this particular night I was tired and wanted to collapse in bed myself. It had been a long day and I was feeling a bit edgy.

OK, I'll be honest. I was feeling more than a "bit" edgy. I was feeling irritable and impatient. I didn't want to answer another question or listen to one more complaint. In fact, I didn't even want to be touched. I just wanted to go away somewhere and be alone.

So, when Elizabeth approached me and asked, "Do you want to play 'Aggravation' with me?" (No kidding. That's really the name of the game she wanted to play. Ironic, huh?) I immediately thought, "No!" Instead of answering, though, I put her off with some excuse so that I could think for a minute first.

What came to my mind? I thought, "How can I be writing a book about becoming holy when I'm still struggling so much with my attitude and angry spirit?" In that moment, I wanted to *want* to play with Elizabeth. I wanted my attitude to be different, to be joyful. But I was feeling selfish and sour and I thought to pretend otherwise would be hypocritical. And who wants to be a hypocrite?

Then God brought to my mind the sermon I'd heard at church the previous Sunday as well as a similar thing I'd read in **Growing Your Faith**. (I love how the Holy Spirit brings thoughts to us at just the right time!) That "thing" was that we determine the direction of our life by the choices we make. That is, according to the choices we make, we move toward or away from holiness.

Think about it. Every day you make hundreds of choices. You choose how to spend your time, how to spend your money, what to watch, what to read, and what to eat — although any mother will admit her kids' whining, begging, and complaining influence these choices! Nonetheless, the decisions are ultimately yours. You know what is at the heart of each one and each choice, even the ones that may seem insignificant, can be made to the glory of

God. Yes, you can choose to honor God by how you spend your spare time, and you can come closer to reflecting His image by the words you choose to speak.

It seemed crazy to me that my current "dilemma" could come down to something as simple as a choice, but that is exactly what it came down to. I didn't "feel" like playing the game with Elizabeth. I was doing quite well at being aggravated on my own, thank you. However, I realized making the choice to play with her *in spite of my feelings* was the right thing to do.

The choice before me was between selfishness and selflessness, between harshness and kindness, between greed and generosity. I am not saying there isn't a right time to say "no" to playing games, or it is selfish to want to spend time alone, or being kind means always doing what your kids want. For me though, at that moment, those traits were at the heart of my decision.

After I thought it through, the decision became an easier one to make, so I went to find Elizabeth and play the game with her. I'd like to say I had tons of fun playing the game, but that would be a lie. What did happen is Elizabeth had fun, and I was glad for choosing to do what was right.

## Refiner's Fire

As I was continuing along on this journey — sometimes feeling up, sometimes down — God brought me another song to encourage me. I was looking up information on the Internet about refining silver when I came across "Refiner's Fire." I thought, "No kidding?! There's actually a song about it!" I clicked on the link and listened. It really is a beautiful song. I wasn't looking for encouragement through music that day, but God knows what we need and He has a habit of delivering it at just the right time.

A few weeks later in church, my pastor repeated the phrase "set apart for God" during his sermon several times. I couldn't help but think about the song I had been humming for those weeks. As he closed the message and the band began to play, I recognized the tune at once. We have sung it several times since then and I always consider it a special gift from God to me when we sing it. I want to share the words with you:

*Purify my heart*
*Let me be as gold and precious silver*
*Purify my heart*
*Let me be as gold, pure gold*

*Refiner's fire*
*My heart's one desire*
*Is to be holy*
*Set apart for You Lord*
*I choose to be holy*
*Set apart for You my Master*
*Ready to do Your will*

*Purify my heart*
*Cleanse me from within and make me holy*
*Purify my heart*
*Cleanse me from my sin, deep within*

*Refiner's fire*
*My heart's one desire*
*Is to be holy*
*Set apart for You Lord*
*I choose to be holy*
*Set apart for You my Master*
*Ready to do Your will*[1]

I sing that song a lot now — in the shower, in the van, in the grocery store. It has become a prayer for me. I long to be holy, set apart for Him.

## Hope for the future

I remember another time, having a similar struggle with my attitude and being discouraged with my progress. I believed that God was at work in me, but I was disappointed because it didn't seem like I was getting anywhere. It was bedtime, Brian was gone, the kids were crazy and I was feeling frustrated. Though I didn't yell and cry like I would have in the past (Oh! A glimpse of progress!), I was more uptight and unkind than I wanted to be. And I *did* yell, and I *wanted* to run away. But I made it through.

The next morning before school, Elizabeth and Joshua were unusually crazy. Matthew was grumpy. And they were all bickering about what movie they were going to choose that afternoon for movie night. As I listened to them, I was reflecting back on the previous night and asking God, "Why? Why do they have to act like this? Why do I have to go through this frustration? I don't see the point!"

My struggle was with my attitude again, wanting to be kind and loving toward my children, but feeling like I might explode if I had to be surrounded by the craziness much longer.

We always pray before Elizabeth and Joshua leave for school. I felt a little hypocritical calling everyone to prayer because of my bad attitude, but it was time. As Brian prayed for everyone, I prayed silently, "Lord, help me to be Your reflection." What God did next amazed me!

Another one of the gifts I received at the Listening in Christ Retreat was a wonderful little book called **God Calling**. It has readings for each day, marked by the month and day, and though I hadn't picked it up in well over a month, for "some reason" I decided to read it that morning while I ate breakfast.

The entry for that very day said, "Life is a training school. Remember, only the pupil giving great promise of future good work would be so singled out by the Master for strenuous and unwearied discipline, teaching and training. You are asking both of you to be not as hundreds of My followers, nay as many, many thousands, but to be even as those who *reflect me* in all they say and do and are. So, my dear children, take this training, not as harsh, but as the tender loving answer to your petition."[2] [emphasis mine]

God doesn't always answer me this quickly, but I couldn't deny Him speaking to me that morning. I wrote in my journal:

> *Ah, yes! You give me hope! Do You really see potential*
> *in me for future good work? I want to do it! And, yes!*
> *I want to reflect You in all that I say and do and am.*
> *And if this fire, these trails with my children, is what*
> *I must go through for training, then so be it. I choose to*
> *trust You!*

## Patient? Who me?

Someone paid me the nicest compliment the other day. I was at school and went into the office to turn in money for my children's lunches. The woman to whom I needed to give the check was doing some work, so I waited. A student came in, needing her assistance so she took care of him while I stood there. She was doing her job and I was in no hurry, so I really didn't mind waiting. After a few minutes she turned around and said, "Are you waiting for me? You're so patient!"

At that last comment, I almost turned around to see if she was talking to someone behind me, or at least so she wouldn't see me laughing. I have never considered myself to be extremely patient. It has occurred to me, though, that when I'm not with my kids, I am able to practice a greater amount of patience than what used to be true of me.

Have you noticed that phenomenon? I notice it especially at the grocery store. With all the kids in school now, I get to go grocery shopping by myself. I have found that people can cut me off, leave their cart in the middle of the isle, or just move slowly in front of me and I handle the "inconvenience" with much greater patience than I used to. Long checkout lines don't even bother me so much anymore.

Certainly, part of my calm in these situations can be attributed to the fact that I am shopping *alone* and haven't been saying, "no," to a steady stream of, "Can we get?" for the past hour. As I have thought about this change in my behavior, however, I am convinced it is further evidence God is transforming me, and that He's using my children to do it.

Do you occasionally hear people say things about you, and find yourself surprised at their evaluation? Just like I was taken back by the comment, "You're so patient," it may be difficult to see your own progress sometimes, but surely other people will notice.

It's like when Grandma says to your child, "Oh, my! You've grown so much!" And you think to yourself, "She looks just the same as she did yesterday." Well, of course you don't notice how much she's grown because you see her every day. But to someone who gets a view only once in awhile, the growth is remarkable.

So it is with your growth in character and holiness. You are intimately aware of the constant struggle, which in itself may impede your view of the progress. Besides, you "see yourself" every day. I want to encourage you to listen to the words of those around you. Listen for encouragement from people who might not even realize they're speaking life and hope into you.

## Peace in the fire

I saw another picture of progress a few days after Matthew started going to kindergarten. When he got home one afternoon, he got into trouble and I made him take a time out. He sat there crying and yelling that it "wasn't fair."

On the one hand I wanted to go into a mini-lecture on the meaning of "fair," but I decided against it. I realized he was tired (his little body needed to adjust to going to school in the afternoon), and so I prayed that God would help him make the adjustment to his new schedule. I prayed and asked God to help Matthew learn to behave better. And I asked God to help me remain calm for the duration of his time out.

When all was said and done I realized, not only did I remain calm during that episode, I actually felt *peaceful*. This realization was *huge* to me. For so long, I had been wanting to reflect Jesus to my children. However, when things got stressful around me, when my kids started whining and misbehaving, or when something happened to irritate me, I tended to snap or at least take on a foul attitude.

But this time things had been different. Matthew was whining, complaining, and sometimes yelling and crying. Instead of mirroring his behavior, however, I was sitting there with him praying for him, loving him, and truly feeling compassion for him. This change of heart was so unusual for me!

As I considered that situation the next day, I gave thanks to God for such a wonderful experience with Him, for the hope that He was transforming me, and for the joy of truly feeling peaceful in the middle of the fire.

## Get up and walk

I have been reading through and meditating on the Gospel of Mark using a method of meditation Jenni taught me called *lectio divina*. Briefly, lectio divina (which is Latin for divine word or divine reading) is the practice of slowly reading a portion of scripture aloud several times and paying attention for a word or image that stands out to you. After you consider all you know about the word or image, you read the passage again asking God, "How does this word (or image) intersect with my life today?" You then wait for God to respond.

I was going through Mark 2:1-12, reading the account of Jesus healing the paralytic who was lowered through the roof by his friends. It seems sometimes we can become so familiar with stories in the Bible that we miss out on the wonder of the truth and what God may want to say to us. As I approached this portion of scripture, I admit, I had the attitude, "Yeah, I know this story. It's a nice story, but what has it got to do with me?" But I asked God, "What does Your word have for me today?" I was amazed at His response.

> "Some men came, bringing to him a paralytic, carried by four of them. Since they could not get him to Jesus because of the crowd, they made an opening in the roof above Jesus and, after digging through it, lowered the mat the paralyzed man was lying on."
>
> Mark 2:3-4

*Paralyzed.* That was the word that stood out to me. But why? I wasn't paralyzed. Or was I? I looked up "paralysis" and "paralyze" in the dictionary. It said, "...the loss of the ability to move," and "to make powerless or ineffective." I thought about the way I'd been feeling, particularly the previous day, and realized that maybe I *was* paralyzed.

I had been angry, short-tempered, selfish and self-centered. I was *not* kind, compassionate, joyful, or anything close to it. At times, I had snapped at my children, been unloving towards my husband, even impatient with my neighbors. God had given me opportunities to practice being kind and gentle and I had turned my back on them. As I evaluated myself, I realized my sin and felt discouraged. I deeply desired to change, but kept thinking, "This is who I am. Is there no hope?"

In my pocket, I had been carrying the scripture verse, "And we pray this in order that you may live a life worthy of the Lord and may please him in every way: bearing fruit in every good work, growing in the knowledge of God." (Colossians 1:10) I realized

I was so far from living a life pleasing to God that I didn't like who I was. I knew I wanted to change, but I felt stuck in this rut of muck and mire called "self."

As I considered "paralyzed" further, I began to agree. I thought, "Yes. I was feeling unable to move forward, closer to God, closer to who He wants me to be. *Paralyzed.*"

But in Mark 2, Jesus says to the paralytic, "Son, your sins are forgiven." Jesus proved He has the authority to forgive sins, and the paralytic got up, took his mat and walked. As I read those words and considered that truth, I thought, "Thank You, Jesus! I am forgiven!" I don't need to be stuck in my self, paralyzed by my sin, unable to become who He wants me to be. He forgives me time and again, and allows me to get up and walk. I am so thankful for my Savior!

That day, the scripture I carried in my pocket was Mark 2:5b&11, "Son, your sins are forgiven...I tell you, get up, take your mat and go home."

## All aboard?

As I am growing in the fire, I am learning that struggling is an important part of growth. Without the struggle there is nothing to overcome and, therefore, no growth. Yet I often get discouraged because I want to be perfect *now*. I don't want to be irritable and impatient with my kids. I don't want to lose my temper and yell at them. But sometimes I *am*, and sometimes I *do*. It's at those times I get upset with myself and climb aboard the guilt train.

As mothers — even "Christian" mothers — it is so easy for us to board the guilt train. We want to do everything just right, but we simply don't perform perfectly. We want to "be there" all the time for our children to prevent every tumble and scratch, but we can't. We want to be sweet and kind to everyone who comes our way, but sometimes we snap. And then we start feeling guilty.

Thoughts like, "I'm not good enough," or "My kids deserve someone better!" start creeping into our minds. Before you know it, you can become stuck in this mode of self-loathing. It paralyzes you. But Jesus can set you free! He forgives your sin, makes up for what you lack, and allows you to walk again. It's time to get off the train!

God is so gracious. When I'm riding on the guilt train, He reaches down and lifts me off. He may do it through His Word, like He did with the passage from Mark 2. Often, however, He uses my husband to assist me in the de-boarding process.

When Brian notices – by his own observation or my confession – that I'm stuck in feelings of guilt, he asks me a simple question, "Where's the grace?" By asking me this simple question, he gently reminds me that I'm *not* perfect. We talk about the fact that God loves me just as much now as He will when I am fully refined. Brian encourages me to live in view of God's perfect love instead of my love of perfection. God knew what He was doing when He brought Brian into my life!

## Sin vs. guilt: You decide

I think it is appropriate here to pause for a discussion about the difference between discontentment with sin and useless guilt. At the start of this chapter I cheered for discontentment with sin. When you draw near to God, you realize more clearly your sin and because you are becoming more like Him, you begin to hate the sin.

You recognize the ways you are *not* Christ-like and that disturbs you. You long to be changed, to be like Him. That is a good thing! I think it is a sure sign of spiritual maturity and growth toward holiness.

Guilt about imperfections, on the other hand, is a useless waste of time and emotion. Instead of drawing near to God and receiving the grace He offers, you focus on an unrealistic ideal.

Realizing you don't measure up to that ideal, you begin to hate yourself. You recognize the ways you are not like June Cleaver and that disturbs you. You long to be changed, but the longing produced by guilt is not a longing for holiness as much as it is a longing for man-centered perfection. This is *not* a good thing.

I think about God calling us higher — wooing us into His kingdom — and filling us with the desire to glorify Him. He does this by lifting our heads up to focus on Him and giving us a desire to please Him. Never in a million years would I believe God would try to motivate us to pursue Him by causing us to detest who we are.

Healthy discontentment with sin is good; pursue it, and the God who is calling you. However, you need to flee from harmful fixation with guilt. If you recognize that you've been riding the guilt train, *please don't allow yourself to start feeling guilty for feeling guilty!!!!*

## Joy in mothering

I mentioned earlier that, for a time, I believed as long as I was a mother of young children I would never really know peace and joy. I thought as long as there was arguing and whining — as long as my little ones were needy — I was going to be stuck fixing problems and meeting demands.

I had hope "one day" things would be better, but my attitude was one of "grin and bear it." God has demonstrated to me, however, that I *can* know peace now; there *is* joy to be had *now*.

I have shared my struggles with you. You know they're real. But the growth is just as real, and God gives me peace and joy in those victories. He gives me joy, too, in the little things my children do — Matthew's spontaneous hugs and kisses, Joshua's love notes, Elizabeth's prayers.

Perhaps my eyes were closed before, or maybe it was the blinders I was wearing which were preventing me from seeing the beautiful things around me. God has shown me there are good things for me to experience *today* and I am so thankful!

Do you remember Tammy, the mother I introduced earlier, who was struggling with issues of anger? She and I talked about this concept of missing joy in our mothering and she shared the following story with me.

Anger had been creeping around her life, and she was stressed. One night, after a day of struggling, she went into her son's room to look at him before she went to bed. Although he was half asleep, he reached up and gave her a big hug. Tammy said, "I was overwhelmed with emotion and knew God was sending His love to me through Justin. I sensed God was saying to me that I had somehow lost the joy of mothering. I cried and I prayed that He would help me to find joy again."

A few days after that incident, I was the speaker at her MOPS group and I shared about my own struggles and the hope I've found. Tammy told me, "Again, I felt God's love in a powerful way because He brought someone to me who understood exactly what I was going through."

My point is this: Even in the midst of our trials, God shows us His love. If we will just believe it is true and be watchful, God will bring us joy in our sorrow.

## Eternal Joy

I would be remiss if I stopped the discussion of joy in mothering, in *anything*, without addressing the Real Source of joy. Just as your children will do things to drive you crazy, they will also do things to fill your heart with pleasure. The same is true of your husband, your friends, your parents, your neighbors and every other living creature on earth. Sometimes people irritate you, and sometimes they delight you.

God will use these individuals in your life to bring you *moments* of joy, but true and lasting joy comes only from Jesus. Jesus left the glory of heaven to come to earth in the form of a man, differing from us only in the fact that He was sinless. He died a criminal's death to pay the debt for our sin, so we could be forgiven. And He rose from the dead and returned to heaven to make a way for us to be reconciled to God. All we need to do is turn from our sin and receive Him as our Savior.

I love the way someone has summarized this transaction: God gave Jesus what *we* deserved, so He could give us what *Jesus* deserved.

Therein is the true and lasting joy we desire. No matter what trials you face or fires you endure, nothing can take away the joy of an eternal relationship with God through Jesus Christ!

*Much of my growth has come and many of my insights have been as a direct result of the quiet time I spend in God's presence. In Appendix B I have shared some ideas that may be helpful to you in your own quiet times.*

## Reflection Questions:

1. As you are pursuing holiness, with what do you continue to struggle?

2. What examples of progress do you see?

3. Do you understand the difference between discontentment with sin and guilt over our imperfections? Have you been riding the guilt train? How can understanding and receiving God's grace help you get off of it?

4. What are some of the things God does or shows you that give you peace and joy *today?*

5. Do you have an eternal relationship with God through Jesus Christ?

*⤳ Chapter Eight ⤳*

# Lessons From the Fire

"GOD IS GOOD, ALL THE TIME. *All the time, God is good.*" My friend, Belinda, frequently makes this statement. Belinda is the Director of Elementary Ministries at my church. I have seen her teaching the kids this statement. She gets up on the stage and says, "God is good!" and the kids respond, "All the time!" Then Belinda says, "All the time," and the kids reply, "God is good!"

## God is good

"God is good, all the time. All the time, God is good," is a truth I wish I had learned when I was in elementary school. For me though, it is a truth I learned from living in the refining fire. Actually, more than learning it on my own, it is a truth I have frequently observed by the fires that other people have endured.

## September 11, 2001

I was at home when Brian called to ask me if I was watching the news. I thought to myself, "It's the middle of the day. Why would I be watching the news?"

When he told me what was happening, I turned on the TV just in time to witness the second tower of the World Trade Center falling to the ground. I couldn't believe what I was seeing!

I heard the report of the plane that went down in Pennsylvania and thought, "Oh, no. They're coming closer to Michigan." When I took my daughter to kindergarten in the afternoon, I noticed a car in the parking lot with someone sitting inside and I wondered if they were up to no good. I was scared. And *paranoid*.

That night as my husband and I were reviewing the events which had transpired during the day, Brian said, "God is still on the throne." God is still on the throne? I didn't understand what he meant. That seemed like such an odd thing to say.

Over the years, as I have experienced my own fires (though, certainly nothing like what the families of the 9/11 victims have lived through) and as I have seen friends go through their own, the statement, "God is still on the throne," has made more sense to me. It goes right along with "God is good, all the time. All the time, God is good."

> Consider these verses:
> *"Jesus Christ is the same yesterday and today and forever."* Hebrews 13:8
> *"[God] does not change like shifting shadows."* James 1:17
> *"I the Lord do not change."* Malachi 3:6
> *"You are good, and what you do is good."* Psalm 119:68

If God never changes, if He is good and what He does is good, then it makes sense that even when tragedies or hardships come upon us, we can trust He is still on His throne. The difficulties we face do not stop God from being God. He does not stop being good, doing good, or loving His creation when it seems our circumstances have gone awry.

I do not mean to trivialize any fire you may have gone through. What I do want to emphasize is one of the greatest lessons I have learned in going through my own fires: *God is good and will never change.*

When I am in a difficult circumstance or when I am praying for someone else who is going through a fire, my first prayer is that God would give the assurance He isn't changing. When our situation is in turmoil — whether on a health, financial or relational level — when we don't know what is going to happen tomorrow, the one thing we can cling to is that God will still be the same. He will be good. He will be reigning from His throne. He will be loving us.

## Jenni's story

Jenni, my mentor, knows this lesson well. Her daughter, Rachel, was diagnosed with stage-four neuro-blastoma at the tender age of three. Her doctors gave her a bleak 20 percent chance for survival.

After they discovered tumors in Rachel's large sinus cavity and adrenal gland, she underwent surgery to remove the adrenal gland, followed by radiation treatments and chemotherapy. Ultimately, she had a stem cell transplant which included total body radiation in hopes of killing any remaining cancer cells in her body.

Rachel was in the hospital for a month during this transplant procedure. The cancer then went into remission and she only had to go to the hospital for follow up appointments.

Although the cancer wasn't bothering her anymore, Rachel suffered many side effects from her treatments. Her hair never grew back. She developed cataracts in her eyes and had to have lens implants. She had ear tube surgeries. Her endocrine system began having problems, requiring her to be put on growth hormone treatments and thyroid supplements. Still, she was cancer-free.

Five years after the transplant, however, Rachel's doctor wanted to have a bone marrow biopsy performed because her blood counts were low. The biopsy came back showing that Rachel had pre-leukemia as a result of the previous cancer treatment. She was going to need a bone marrow transplant, using someone else's bone marrow.

The doctors only gave Rachel a 10 percent chance for survival from this procedure, but said if she survived the transplant, she wouldn't relapse. Rachel spent over a month in the hospital with this transplant and the procedure was even more dreadful than the first one. Rachel ended up in the ICU due to a bad lung problem and had to be put on a ventilator. Jenni thought her precious daughter was going to die.

At the time there was an experimental drug being used to treat lung conditions like the one Rachel had developed. It just so "happened" that Rachel was at one of the two hospitals in the entire country which was participating in this clinical trial. In spite of the drug being permitted only for adults, Rachel was allowed to receive it because her condition was life-threatening. Within 36 hours of getting the drug, she was ready to have the ventilator removed. She went home a week later.

It has been four years since that transplant. Rachel is now on ten different medications and has a feeding tube. She is dealing with mild rejection of the bone marrow, but the medicines are meant to help her body accept the marrow. So far she hasn't been growing and doesn't seem to be responding to the growth hormone treatments. Although she isn't sick anymore, Jenni says she isn't healthy either. The doctors do give Jenni hope though that eventually the rejection of the marrow will come to an end.

In reflecting on what she has been through and considering what God has taught her, Jenni is still convinced that God is good. She said, "Some circumstances will tell you, 'Well, God can't be good if He lets this happen.' I think the biggest impact Rachel's illness has had on me as a mother and a child of God is that I have come to have an eternal perspective on life. I understand and trust more deeply in God's wisdom, power, and love over all of life's twists and turns. When I don't understand the 'Why did this happen?' or 'How can this be best for her?' I choose to believe that God is good and He knows what is best for her."

Jenni is firmly grounded in the Word of God. She knows it and draws her strength from it, even when her circumstances seem to scream the opposite. Because she knows His Word and trusts that He is good, when she does not understand what's going on, when her circumstances do not make sense to her, she trusts Him.

This fire in Jenni's life has been going on for eleven years. Through it, God has given Jenni strength and understanding and increased her faith in who He is. She recognizes that she doesn't see with God's perspective and has learned to trust in His plan instead of looking for answers in her own view. She says, "God knows what is going to last in eternity. And I've come to realize that sometimes what I consider a curse, He sees as a blessing."

Do you understand why I love having Jenni as my mentor? Her faith builds *my* faith. That's why I strongly urge you to consider finding a mentor if you don't have one already!

## A purpose for everything

As I have gone through trials and witnessed others going through them, I've realized that not all fires are the same. Some fires are very hot and are often accompanied by pain, while others are good for providing warmth and comfort. God has taught me another valuable lesson as I have seen Him use these different fires: *There is a purpose for everything that happens in our lives.*

## Joseph's story

When I think of this lesson — that in God's economy there are no random or chance events — I am reminded of the story of Joseph in the book of Genesis. His father favored Joseph over his brothers, so they hated him. He had these crazy dreams about his brothers, and even his mother and father, bowing down to him. And the brothers' hatred grew and intensified.

When Joseph's father sent him to check on his brothers and their flocks one day, they recognized him in the distance and plotted to kill him. They changed their minds, however, and sold him instead to a passing caravan of traders.

Joseph was taken to Egypt and sold to Potiphar, one of Pharaoh's officials. Joseph was favored by Potiphar and became his attendant, but when Potiphar's wife lied and said that Joseph had tried to seduce her, Potiphar had him thrown into jail.

In jail, Joseph met a couple of guys and interpreted some dreams. These interactions eventually led to Joseph interpreting dreams for Pharaoh, as God revealed the meanings to him. Following Joseph's display of God's power, he was put in charge of the whole land of Egypt and was ultimately used to save the people from a severe famine.

In time, Joseph's brothers came to him (not knowing he was their brother) seeking food. When Joseph revealed his true identity to his brothers, they were terrified because of what they had done to him. But Joseph, understanding what *God* had done, explained to his brothers, "It was not you who sent me here, but God." (Genesis 45:8)

How many "random" occurrences were there in Joseph's life? *Every single one* was used by God to accomplish His purpose.

I like the way Ruth Meyers communicates this truth in **31 Days of Praise**. She writes, "I praise You for Your sovereignty over the broad events of my life and over the details. With You, nothing is accidental, nothing is incidental, and no experience is wasted... And every trial that You allow to happen is a platform on which You reveal Yourself, showing Your love and power, both to me and to others looking on."[1]

What do you think of the statement that "nothing in our lives is accidental, incidental or wasted"?

To me, it says a lot about who God is, and how big He is. He knows everything about you. He is intimately aware of everything that is happening in your life. And in His wisdom He knows how to work it all together for your good.

## Nikki's story

I want to introduce you to my sister-in-law, Nikki. I first met Nikki 17 years ago. This is how she describes the way she was then: "I was critical and judgmental of myself and everyone that was around me. I was a perfectionist. I had to be the best at every thing: the best girlfriend, the best friend, the best worker. The worst thing about me was I was completely unforgiving. No grace at all.

"I was a chameleon. I was so unhappy with who I was, lacked so much confidence, that I would change and be the person I thought others wanted me to be. It was so tiring trying to be so many people at one time."

Now she says, "At age 36, I have finally become a person who can say, 'I like who I am, where I am in life, and where I am going.'" Talk about a major turn around!

The first time I heard Nikki say she likes who she is becoming, I remember a real sense of joy coming over me. This woman who once was very bitter and cold (I love you, Nikki, but you were!) actually said *she liked herself!*

I asked Nikki to share her story with me so I could share it with *you*. I think it is absolutely awesome to consider God's sovereignty over the broad events and the details of Nikki's life. When I think about the journey she has been on, my faith that there is a purpose for everything which happens in our lives is strengthened. I hope your faith will also increase.

Seventeen years ago, Nikki was in a great amount of turmoil. She had ended a 4 ½ year long relationship, was no longer on speaking terms with her best friend, and to top it all off, she'd just gotten "the talk" from her boss about changes she needed to make if she intended to keep her job.

The despair Nikki was in as a result of these events drove her to her knees. She poured her heart out to Jesus. Nikki asked Him to take away her pain, her loneliness, and her emptiness, and she invited Him into her life. God had used those events to draw Nikki to Himself.

In time, God restored those things that were troubling Nikki. She was promoted at work, got reconnected with her friend and through that friend she met Jeff, the man she later married. Although she was saved, Nikki remained skeptical of "religion" and told her boyfriend (now husband) she would never attend or join a church. But God knew better!

When Jeff and Nikki were married, God brought new hope into her life. He surrounded Nikki with an extended family that accepted her, prayed for her, and cared enough about her to be patient as she discovered a deeper relationship with Him. She recognizes these relationships as a significant aspect of her journey toward being able to say she likes herself.

Then she started having children...and you *know* God uses motherhood to bring a woman nearer to Himself. As you may understand — perhaps from personal experience — after Nikki's first daughter was born, her conversations with God became much more frequent than they had ever been.

She says, "She would cry, I would cry, and we would pray to Jesus. He was on my mind's speed dial, so to speak. Before bottles, before naps, for minor discomforts, for allowing her to wake, for the smile she just gave. You name it, I was praying to or praising God." Nikki was growing, but God still had more He wanted to do.

Jeff and Nikki decided they wanted to move closer to Jeff's work. They bought a house, Nikki quit her job, and they moved. Their lives were changed — especially because Nikki became a stay-at-home-mom! And God used another series of events to draw her even closer to Himself.

In spite of some difficulty and disappointment, Jeff and Nikki found a church they wanted to attend. (Remember when Nikki said she'd never attend church?) This church had a MOPS group and, knowing she needed to surround herself with women who knew and loved the Lord, she filled out and sent in an application. God knew she needed to be there, too, and her application was accepted.

I'll let Nikki finish the story:

"Jesus led me to this amazing group of women and through them and the MOPS ministry, I started to feel 'connected' to the church. I found myself wanting to get involved and wanting to hear the next message. I was falling even deeper in love with Jesus Christ and was realizing that my relationship with Him was just in its infancy.

"As I was discovering Jesus, the church 'home' and becoming more involved in the MOPS group, I was becoming an increasingly happier person, feeling so much more fulfilled spiritually.

"The crazy part is *other* people were starting to make comments that I guarantee you I wouldn't have received seventeen years ago. Comments about what a nice person I am. Comments about what a happy and thoughtful person I am. Comments that made me feel proud."

Can you see how God was using the events in Nikki's life to work out His purposes? (Not that He is finished with her yet – and I know Nikki would agree.) He used turmoil as well as "good" things, He brought people into her life to love her, and He used change in relationships and living situations. Sometimes the fires in Nikki's life were very hot and other times they just kept her comfortable. God used *each one* according to His purposes.

## My story

What about something as "random" as where you live when you're four years old? Is God really concerned with that detail, too? I believe so, and I'll tell you why.

When I was four years old, my mom and dad wanted to move our family into a bigger house. I remember driving by the property on which my parents wanted to build a house for us. It was in a nice neighborhood, and right next door to their good friends. After receiving the quote from the contractor, though, my dad decided building a house was too expensive. Mom really wanted a *new* house, but it just wasn't going to happen.

Instead they found and bought a house in a different neighborhood. The neighborhood into which we moved was less than a mile away from the one into which we were *going* to move, but it crossed the district line which determined the schools I would attend from kindergarten through eighth grade.

At first glance, these things may seem insignificant. Regardless of where I lived and attended school, I learned to read and write. I know how to add, subtract, multiply and divide. So what's the difference?

The difference is, the friends I made and the experiences I had at Hayes Elementary and Middle Schools were not the same as the ones I would have had at Neff Elementary and Beagle Middle Schools.

I remember Mrs. Rolinson, my music teacher in elementary school. I thought she was so pretty, with her long blonde hair. Her voice was kind and gentle and I loved going to music class. She taught us fun songs and I am confident she was the one who instilled in me a love for singing.

Singing would prove to be a significant influencer in my life. In middle school, I was in a musical production and I joined the choir. I found so much joy in these activities that I continued to pursue them in high school, participating in numerous musicals and choirs.

Somewhere in the midst of the singing, I decided that I wanted to study music in college. (Actually, I wanted to become a Broadway star, but my parents wanted me to get an education "just in case"...) So when it came time to choose where I would attend college, I really had an easy decision to make. My choir teacher, Mrs. Lange — who also had a tremendous impact on my life — advised me that Western Michigan University was the best place for me to go. She said their music department was fantastic, and that's all it took for me. I was going to be a Bronco!

It was at WMU, living in Smith Burnham Hall, that I met Brian Hossink. He thought I was cute, so he joined my committee on Hall Council, and I thought he was cute so I stopped by to visit when he was working at the reception desk.

Over time, we started dating. He asked me questions about Christianity and my faith. He read the Bible with me and through his witness I realized I was *not* a Christian! But he told me how I could be. God used Brian to bring me into a saving relationship with Himself.

And, yes, about four years later I married him!

I have often wondered, "What if we had moved into that other neighborhood when I was four years old?" Would I have developed a love for music, gone to WMU, met Brian and, through him, met God?

My mom didn't get the new house she wanted, but I am so thankful for the path my life took as a result. I was just talking to my mom about the reason for my parents' decision to buy instead of build. She said, "You know, there's a reason for everything." Yes, Mom, you're right again. (Please tell me someday our kids will say those words to us!)

As it turns out, I think the music was also just a stepping stone God used to get me to WMU and Himself. After about nine weeks of college, doing *nothing* but music, I realized I was beginning to hate it. And I liked it too much to hate it, so I changed my major and put Broadway thoughts away for good.

God had given me a new life here on earth and the promise for an eternity brighter than any lights on Broadway could ever dream of being!

A house, a school, a couple of music teachers, a love for singing, a university, a cute college freshman. Seemingly simple, insignificant events? *Not a chance!* God used each one of them perfectly to bring me to Himself.

## Choosing to trust

It is because of the fact God doesn't allow any of our experiences to be wasted that I feel it is fair for me to ask Him, "God, what is it You want to work in me right now?" I believe He will use *everything*, and I want to participate in what He's doing.

On those occasions when He shows me what He's doing, I am filled with joy to know that He's at work. Other times, I don't understand and I just need to choose to trust Him.

My mom shared with me that she and my dad are having one of those times now. They've been trying to sell their cottage for a couple of years. Even though they've had people who they *thought* were going to buy it, it still sits "For Sale" and they're getting tired. But she faithfully maintains, "There's a reason for everything."

One of those "other times" for me has been dragging on for nearly two years. I debated about whether or not to include this example, but I trust if you meet Matthew some day when he's a vulnerable adolescent, you won't tease him with your "inside knowledge."

Matthew is six years old and for almost two years now, he has been wetting or soiling his pants almost daily. We have taken him to doctors. We have rewarded him with stickers on the calendar. We have taken away privileges. We have given him incentives. You name it — we've tried it.

He might go a few days without an accident, and then a few days with several accidents each day. I see absolutely no rhyme or reason to this behavior and I am *tired*.

On several occasions I have begged God to show me what the purpose of these accidents is. I have yet to receive an answer on this one, so I have made the decision to just trust that God knows what He's doing.

I wrote about this decision in my journal:

> *Thank You that You are working Your will in me.*
> *Thank You that You are in control even when I don't*
> *understand — when I can't see or make sense of a*
> *situation, when You seem hidden to me — still You are*
> *in control and are working all these things for good.*
>
> *Lord, if only I would always remember Who is in*
> *charge — Who is "running this place," — then I would*
> *not worry or fret. You are <u>good always</u>. You are <u>sovereign</u>*
> *<u>always</u>. You deserve my <u>praise always</u>.*
>
> *And I praise You!*

By experience and observation, these are the lessons I have learned in the fire: *God is good, all the time. All the time, God is good.* And, *there is a purpose for everything that happens in our lives.*

As you journey through life, in and out of various fires, I pray these lessons will buoy you and build your faith.

Think about this: It isn't a random chance that you're reading this book! God knew you would be reading these words before I even knew I'd be writing them. He is always good and He will use *everything* in your life according to His good purposes!

# Reflection Questions:

1. Do you believe that God is always good?

2. How can you reconcile God's goodness with earthly tragedy and heartbreak?

3. How has knowing that God is always good carried you through painful times?

4. What is your response to the statement, "With [God] nothing is accidental, nothing is incidental and no experience is wasted?"

5. What are some experiences in your life that may *seem* to be insignificant, but that you realize God has used in significant ways?

~ *Chapter Nine* ~

# Hope From the Fire

THIS PROCESS OF TRANSFORMATION has been a wonderful, yet difficult journey; God has taught me so much along the way. It has been wonderful because He has given me hope. The little victories I've experienced give me courage to carry on. The journey has been difficult, however, *because* of the trials I've needed to go through in order to experience the small victories.

I am a broken woman who would much rather have holiness handed to her on a platter — *a silver one* — than to have to go through the process of transformation. Yet, I have grown in my confidence that God is good *all* the time and He is using the hard times in my life to transform me.

## Hope in the hard times

The truth which tells me God is transforming me through trials is the first piece of hope I'm taking from the fire. In the last chapter, I spoke very generally about the lesson I've learned that God uses *everything* in our lives for His purposes. Now I want to focus specifically on the hope I have that He uses the *hard times* to transform us.

Certainly, God will use good days, moments of joy, and times when "all is well" with our circumstance to accomplish good things. But I firmly believe it is the hard times, the pain and confusion which He uses for the purpose of growing us. It's like when Brian has been to the gym and moans the next day as he walks, "Oh! I had a good legs work-out yesterday!" That statement means he is presently in quite a bit of pain, but he knows his muscles are getting stronger and firmer and he likes that. (So do I!)

I like what Jerry Bridges said about God using the hard times. Referring to serious *and* trivial hardships he wrote, "all of these circumstances and events are intended by God to be means of developing more Christ-like character."[1]

Do you see the hope in those words? When you are at your wits' end, when you aren't sure how you're going to make it through the day, when you're experiencing more pain and heartache than you thought possible, or even when you're dealing with a minor annoyance, *God is giving you the chance to become more like Jesus.*

It's easy to be peaceful, joyful and overflowing with love when life is smooth. God knows we need the hard times to grow.

Jerry Bridges made another statement about God using the hard times in our lives to transform us that was meaningful to me. He wrote: "[God] doesn't have to debate with Himself over what is most suitable for us. He knows intuitively and perfectly the nature, intensity, and duration of adversity that will best serve His purpose to make us partakers of His holiness."[2]

As God so often does, He timed my reading of this statement perfectly. Just the day before, I was wondering how to handle a certain situation with Matthew. Do I do this, or that? What would be fair? What would be effective? Will it change his behavior? Is five hours in "time out" too much?

Brian! Help! I had debated with myself, and now I needed to call a conference. In that particular case, two heads *weren't* better than one. Even after hashing out the situation with my husband,

I couldn't figure out how to best handle it. Then I pondered the idea that God "doesn't have to debate with Himself." How wonderful is that!

God knows *exactly* what is needed in your life to make you holy. Those hard times you've been going through, they aren't there by mistake. It isn't as though God is sitting up in heaven listening to the angels singing and when He glances down at you He says in shock, **"Oh my! Look what's going on in that dear woman's life. I sure hope she can handle that situation. I wonder if it's going to be too much. Maybe I should do something about it for her. What if she gets mad at Me and thinks I'm mean? What if I allow her to go through this whole thing and find out it wasn't the right approach to shaping her at all?"** Sounds a bit ridiculous, doesn't it?

I imagine it a bit differently. I picture God sitting in heaven listening to the angels singing, with a faithful and constant eye fixed upon you, upon each of us, and His conversation is more like this: **"I see you. I know what you're going through. I hear your cry for help and My Spirit is there with you now, as He always has been. O, dear one, I love you so much. The day will come when you will understand the reason for these trails. Do you realize that I'm using them to make you more like My Beloved Son? You are going to be so beautiful!**

**"I understand that you don't think you can take this situation much longer. Trust Me, beloved. I know what is necessary to make you holy. I will not destroy you or allow you to be destroyed. I am using this trial like a fire to refine and purify you. It is for your good, dear one. Trust Me!"**

I heard a speaker say once, "Don't despise what you're going through." When I considered her statement in light of my mothering struggles, I thought, "Yeah, right." Now I can say, "While I might not *like* what I'm going through, if God is using it to make me more like Him, then I *won't* despise it."

I hope as you consider your own hard times you, too, are becoming convinced God is using them to make you into the woman He wants you to be. And I pray that you will take this piece of hope from the fire and will be able to say you do not despise what you're going through either.

## Hope in His presence

The second piece of hope I have taken from this refining fire is that God is always with me, even during the hard times.

I am convinced I am forever in His care. He doesn't take this cake of silver named Karen, whom He has carefully mined and washed and smelted, throw her in the furnace and then walk away only to come back in a day or two to find silver ash floating around.

Rather, I am confident He is intimately involved in every aspect of my life, always present, always listening, always able to care for me. The amazing thing to me is He is just as present in *your* life, all the while He is holding the universe together and watching over the birds of the air and the flowers of the field.

Isaiah 41:13 says, "For I am the Lord, your God, who takes you by the right hand and says to you, 'Do not fear, I will help you.'" It makes such a difference to me, knowing God is with me in each of my trials. I am never alone.

Last summer my family and I were visiting my mom and dad. It was time for dinner and as I was rounding up the kids, I noticed Matthew had wet his pants. I got clean pants for him and told him to put them on.

By this time, Elizabeth and Joshua were already upstairs. Matthew was hungry and he just wanted to eat dinner. I told him he needed to change his pants first. He was also tired and a bit irrational and he just stood at the bottom of the stairs and cried while we went back and forth about him changing his pants before he ate dinner. I thought what I was asking him to do was a pretty simple thing and I was getting frustrated with him. Honestly, I wanted to leave him there crying until he came to his senses!

Then I remembered that God was with me, and I asked Him, "How do *You* respond to *me* when I am in Matthew's position?" The answer wasn't too difficult to figure out. When *I* am being childish and irrational, God doesn't respond to me out of frustration.

No, in love, He has pity on me and tends to my need. So that's what I did for Matthew. Instead of yelling again, I went to him and *helped* him change his pants. Then I took him upstairs and gave him dinner. And, if I remember right, the rest of the evening was very pleasant.

God was present with me in that time when I was nearing my wits' end. His Spirit gave me the understanding I needed to handle the situation. I am so glad God takes me by the hand and says, **"I will help you."**

The image of God taking us by the hand is wonderful, isn't it? You can't take someone by the hand unless you are very near to them. And when you hold someone's hand, it is a sign you love them. They are safe in your presence. Who hasn't heard a child say, "Hold my hand, Mommy!" when they're afraid?

So it is with you and God. He is very near to you, even in the hard times. He said He would always be with you and He would never leave you. *God doesn't lie!* When your fire is really hot and you're afraid, He is there. Reach for Him. When your situation seems out of control and you don't know what to do, He is there. Call upon Him. When it seems like your trial is going to overtake you and you don't think you can handle it, He is there. Trust Him.

## Hope in His love and faithfulness

The third piece of hope I have taken from the refining fire is a better understanding of God's love and faithfulness. As I've gone through the valleys, I've realized He doesn't just take us *to* them and leave us there, but He goes *through* the valleys with us.

## The widow's oil

The Bible is full of stories of God's faithfulness, but there is one Old Testament story which makes it clearer to me than any other. It is the story in 2 Kings 4 about the woman and her jar of oil.

This woman was a widow and was in debt. Her husband used to serve God and now his creditor was coming to take her sons to be his slaves because she couldn't pay him the money her husband owed.

I can't imagine being in such a situation — to lose my husband and then to face the idea that my children were going to be taken away, too. I imagine that this woman was sad and fearful for herself, contemplating a life completely alone, the ones she loved so dearly having been ripped from her.

Wouldn't she also be afraid for her sons who were going to be taken away and made slaves? Perhaps she was worrying about whether her boys were going to be abused. Who was going to make them their favorite dinner? Who would hug and kiss them good night? What amount of inner turmoil could she have been facing?

So she approached Elisha, the prophet, to seek help. He asked her what she had in her house, to which she replied that she had nothing, except a little oil. How do you suppose she was feeling then?

"Well, Elisha, I have no husband. My sons are going to be taken away from me. And now that you mention it, I really don't have anything else. Just a little oil. I came here for help, but I guess I'm hopeless." But God was holding her.

Elisha gave her instructions to ask all her neighbors for empty jars. He said, "Don't ask for just a few." She was to gather a lot of them. Then she was to go into her house with her sons and *fill* each of the jars with oil. But remember, she said she only had a *little* oil. Even so, she did as Elisha instructed her and the oil didn't stop flowing until the last jar had been filled.

When she was finished, the widow went to Elisha and told him what had happened. He told her to sell the oil and pay her debts, and then she and her sons could live on what was left.

Can you imagine her relief? She had already lost her husband. She was about to lose her sons. And there was literally nothing she could do to save them. But God didn't leave her alone. He made her oil flow so that she could satisfy her financial obligations and still have enough to live on. She saw His faithfulness. *But if she hadn't been in that desperate situation, how would she have known God could take care of her like that?*

Maybe you've never been in a situation quite as desperate as this widow. Maybe you've never experienced something as miraculous as a seemingly endless supply of oil. But I have a suspicion that if you recounted the hard times you've endured and looked for God's hand in them, you would be amazed at the way He faithfully saw you through.

My dad recently had open-heart surgery to correct a condition that was preventing his blood from properly flowing out of his heart. It was a scary time for both him and my mom. Through it, though, he came up with a new life motto: If God takes you to it, He'll take you through it.

No matter if your situation is something as major as open-heart surgery or as minor as a child who keeps wetting his pants, *God is perfectly faithful and He will see you through.*

## Jesus wept

The Bible is full of stories of God's love. There is one in particular that stands out to me when I think of God showing His love through hard times. It is the New Testament story about Mary and Martha and their brother, Lazarus. Lazarus was sick and his sisters sent a message to Jesus telling Him, "Lord, the one you love is sick." (John 11:3) Although Jesus loved Mary and Martha and

Lazarus, when He received the message, He "stayed where He was two more days." (John 11:6) And Lazarus died.

The women were concerned about their sick brother, so they sent word to Jesus and waited. Their brother died, and they waited. People came to mourn with them, and still they waited for Jesus.

How do you think the women were feeling at that point? Certainly they were sad because their brother was dead. Might they have also been confused, perhaps feeling unloved because Jesus hadn't come?

When He did get there, Jesus found Lazarus had been dead for four days! Both Mary and Martha, when they saw Jesus, said to Him, "If you had been here, my brother would not have died." Mary fell at His feet weeping. Then, "Jesus wept." (John 11:35)

When the women saw Jesus weeping, when they saw how deeply moved He was, do you think they questioned His love? Have you ever cared so much about someone and the pain they were in you wept with them? Or, maybe you've experienced someone crying with you when you've been hurting? You *know* that love is real!

However, that isn't the end of the story. Jesus called Lazarus out of the grave. He brought Lazarus back to life! Imagine the rejoicing that happened then! But if Mary and Martha had not gone through their fire, how would they have known God's love and seen His faithfulness as He brought their brother back to life?

### "Karen, I love you!"

Believe it or not, there was a time when I believe God used one of Matthew's "accidents" to tell me He loves me. I don't know how many accidents he'd had already that day, but when I noticed Matthew had wet his pants *again*, I was not happy. I had "had it."

I marched him upstairs to get him into the bathtub. I remember more than being angry, I was feeling some combination of frustration and despair. For over a year, he had been wetting his pants two, three, sometimes even four times a day. And here we were, at it again.

He got undressed and washed out his pants as I fumed around the bathroom, surely grumbling about not wanting to do this again. Matthew got in the tub and as I handed him the washcloth, he looked up into my eyes and said, *"I love you."*

I stopped my fuming and listened. I just let those words soak in. I took it as from God, as though He were saying to me, **"Karen, I know you're tired of this. I know you don't want to do another load of laundry. I know you'd rather be doing something else. I know you want to scream right now. But you're taking care of this little boy and I want you to know that I love you."** I can tell you, my whole demeanor changed.

Once I wondered aloud if I should take every accident Matthew has as a reminder that God loves me. My husband thought that idea sounded entirely too optimistic. He may be right, but sometimes when Matthew wets his pants, I think about it and smile and tell God I love Him, too.

## Otherwise, how would I know?

I have been thinking about this concept of hard times: *trials, fires, valleys.* Any number of words can describe the difficult times we go through. By now you know I'm convinced (and I hope your confidence has grown, too) God uses these times to shape us and make us more like Him. I am so thankful for that work on His part.

As I have gone through my own fires, I have become equally thankful that God uses them simply to cause me to run to and cling to Him. Honestly, if life were "perfect," if I never had a trouble or a care in the world, if I thought I could handle every day depending on my own strength and charm, would I even think I need God?

God is just as good on the days when "all is well" with my circumstances as He is on the days when I feel like I'm going to drown. Nothing about Him changes. What changes is my perspective — from trusting in myself to trusting in the One who made me, who loves me, who knows what is best for me, and who is able to do it.

Going through hard times causes me to run to God. I have come to the place in my life where I know I cannot do this on my own. So I run to Him. And I have found that He is faithful.

When I share this message about God's refining fire with MOPS groups, I usually close by singing one of my favorite songs by Kathy Troccoli. It speaks my heart and I believe it gives hope, so I want to share it with you now. It's called "How Would I Know?"

> *If it wasn't for the times that I was down*
> *If it wasn't for the times that I was bound*
> *For all the times that I wondered*
> *How I would ever make it through*
> *All of the times that I couldn't see my way*
> *And I had to turn to You*
>
> *How would I know You could deliver?*
> *How would I know You could set free?*
> *If there had never been a battle,*
> *How would I know the victory?*
> *How would I know You could be faithful*
> *To meet all of my needs?*
> *Lord, I appreciate the hard times*
> *Otherwise, how would I know?*
>
> *I remember all the times I had to cry*
> *And at the time all I could do was wonder, "Why?"*

*Why would a God so kind and loving*
*Allow me to go through all this pain?*
*If I could see into the future*
*Then I would know the joy I'd gain.*

*But how would I know You could deliver?*
*How would I know You could set free?*
*If there had never been a battle,*
*How would I know the victory?*
*How would I know You could be faithful*
*To meet all of my needs?*
*Lord, I appreciate the hard times*
*Otherwise, how would I know?*

*How would I know that You could*
*Make a way, out of no way?*
*How would I know if I never had a need?*
*[Mother], I know what you're going through*
*Sister, I know cause I've been in your shoes*
*And I can truly say that I know what God can do!*

*But how would I know You could deliver?*
*How would I know You could set free?*
*If there had never been a battle,*
*How would I know the victory?*
*How would I know You could be faithful,*
*To meet all of my needs?*
*Lord, I appreciate the hard times*
*Otherwise how would I know?*[23]

# Then and now

It's been nearly four years since I was stumped by that assignment to write down what I love most about my kids. I had nearly forgotten about it.

It came back to me, however, when I attended an Apples of Gold reunion. The evening was an enjoyable time of fellowship and good food. Before we ended, each of the mentors was given an opportunity to share some parting thoughts. One mentor suggested we review the book and complete any homework assignments we'd left undone. (A telling chuckle crossed the room.) It was in reflecting on her comment that I was greatly encouraged.

I remembered how I was so despairing of motherhood during my six weeks — and following months — of Apples of Gold! Conversations I'd had about receiving the "Meanest Mom in the World" award came back to me. I recalled aching for just an ounce of hope that I would make it through one more day.

Then it occurred to me I couldn't remember the last time Joshua told me I was the "Meanest Mom in the World". It is more common now for him to write me love notes! In fact, sitting in front of me as I write these words is a poster he made to "inspire" me on my writing retreat. It has a big smiley face in the middle and is surrounded by the loving phrases, "You rock!" "My mom is the best!" and "I love you!"

Sure, we still have our moments, but I smile as I recognize that our relationship is much more peaceful now. I realize I am able to write down what I love most about him — *his tender heart.*

Then I think, "Maybe the father of that teenage boy was right. I think Joshua *is* changing."

No. I think we're *both* changing.

Even so, I am painfully aware that I am not finished in the fire. I still get frustrated with my children's immaturity and disobedience. Irritability and impatience still creep into my being.

Sometimes selfish, self-centered "me" takes over my day and leaves me wondering if I'll ever change. Can you relate?

Yet, I am reminded and thankful that God doesn't give up on me even in *my* immaturity and disobedience. This hope is for you too, my friend. He won't give up on you either. Though I know there will still be times of tears, I will trust in God.

Will you join me? Let us *choose* to trust in God — knowing He loves us, knowing He is sovereign and good, and knowing that in the end, *we will be refined like silver.*

# Reflection Questions:

1. What is your response to the statement, "Don't despise what you're going through?"

2. How does it make you feel to know that God is with you always? Even in the hard times?

3. In what ways has God shown His love and faithfulness to you as you've gone through hard times in your life?

## APPENDIX A

# Scripture Verses to Help You

CARRYING SCRIPTURE VERSES AROUND IN MY POCKET has been a wonderful way for me to remember God's presence and to be mindful of His work in my life. I keep a paper cube on the bookshelf by my Bible so when I come across a verse I want to carry with me I don't have to hunt for paper. My hope is that you will adopt some form of this practice and that you will find joy as you sense God speaking His love to you.

If you decide to do this, I trust that God will lead you to the words He wants to speak to you. As a way of getting you started, I would like to share some of the verses I have carried in my pocket.

## To remind me how great God is:

"Your love, O Lord, reaches to the heavens, Your faithfulness to the skies. Your righteousness is like the mighty mountains, Your justice like the great deep. O Lord, You preserve both man and beast. How priceless is Your unfailing love." Psalm 36:5-7a

## To remind me that God is able to handle my needs:

"And God is able to make all grace abound to you, so that always having all sufficiency in everything, you may have an abundance for every good deed." 2 Corinthians 9:8

## When I start to think of myself more highly than I ought:

"Praise be to the Lord God, the God of Israel, who alone does marvelous deeds. Praise be to His glorious name forever; may the whole earth be filled with His glory. Amen and Amen." Psalm 72:18-19

OR

"Not to [me], O Lord, not to [me] but to Your name be the glory, because of Your love and faithfulness." Psalm 115:1

## When I'm praying about something that is heavy on my heart:

"Before they call I will answer; while they are still speaking I will hear." Isaiah 65:24

## On days when I'm feeling worn and weary:

"The Lord your God is with you, He is mighty to save. He will take great delight in you, He will quiet you with His love, He will rejoice over you with singing." Zephaniah 3:17

"Please quiet me with Your love," is often a prayer I whisper when I have this verse in my pocket.

## To remind me that God does have a purpose for me and all the stuff I'm going through:

"For we are God's workmanship, created in Christ Jesus to do good works, which God prepared in advance for us to do." Ephesians 2:10

When I'm going to be alone with the kids:

"When you pass through the waters, I will be with you; and when you pass through the rivers, they will not sweep over you. When you walk through the fire, you will not be burned; the flames will not set you ablaze." Isaiah 43:2

When I know that the day before me is going to be stressful:

"Let the peace of Christ rule in your hearts, since as members of one body you were called to peace. And be thankful." Colossians 3:15

# THE GOSPEL OF MARK

The time I have spent in the Gospel of Mark has produced some great verses for me to reflect on and carry in my pocket.

When I need to be reminded that my sins are forgiven:

"Son, your sins are forgiven...I tell you, get up, take your mat and walk." Mark 2:5b & 11

When I don't understand what God is doing, I can trust that He is working in me:

"Night and day, whether he sleeps or gets up, the seed sprouts and grows, though he does not understand how." Mark 4:27

To remind me to praise Jesus for His abiding presence and to pray throughout the day that His presence would be known:

"Yet he could not keep his presence secret." Mark 7:24b

To encourage me to praise Jesus for His work, and to trust that He is doing a good work in me:

"He has done everything well." Mark 7:37b

When I need to practice being more patient with my children:

"He sighed deeply and said...Then he left them." Mark 8:12a & 13a

When I read this verse, I was struck by Jesus' response in what seemed to me would have been a very frustrating situation. Surely, He must have been upset with the Pharisees, but *He didn't yell at them.*

To remind me no problem is too big, and nothing is too difficult for God:

"But when they looked up, they saw that the stone, which was very large, had been rolled away." Mark 16:4

## APPENDIX B

# Quiet Time Suggestions

**PERHAPS YOU ARE ESTABLISHED** in having quiet times with God, reading the Bible and praying. Maybe, though, you haven't gotten into this practice and you're wondering what to do with the time. Or, perhaps you are in need of some fresh ideas to incorporate into your time with God.

Whatever your situation, as you journey on your own road to holiness, I want to offer some of the things that have been meaningful to me as I seek to know God better and become more like Him.

# Breathing

I mentioned that I often pray "on the go" and when things are crazy around me. Sometimes, though, I need to find time when I can be alone and quiet before the Lord. At these times, one of the ways I like to pray is with a breathing exercise.

I sit in my chair and close my eyes and breathe slowly and deeply. My goal in this time is to fill myself with Jesus and empty myself of "me." As I inhale I say His name to myself, "Jesus," and I pause for just a moment.

On my exhale, which is also slow and deliberate, I name my sin. "Irritability," "Impatience," "Selfishness," "Self righteousness," "Bitterness." I just say whatever comes to mind. And if nothing comes to my mind, I say, "Pride" because I know I have plenty to confess.

So it goes like this. I breathe in and think, "Jesus." As I do this, I imagine Him filling me up and I pause with that image. Then I breathe out and think, "Irritability," and I imagine irritability leaving my body. Inhale, "Jesus." Pause. Exhale, "Impatience." Pause. Inhale, "Jesus." Pause. Exhale, "Selfishness." Pause.

I will sit and pray like this for five or ten minutes. I think about becoming who He wants me to be – filling up on Him and separating myself from my sin. Not only is this a soul cleansing exercise because of the confession, but it builds hope in me that I am becoming more like Him.

Let's be realistic, though. As mothers, we don't always have five or ten minutes when our surroundings are peaceful and we can sit in a chair for a good soul cleansing. Sometimes we need an emergency clean-up job. When I am in one of those situations – when I'm on the verge of either losing it or crying – I stop dead in my tracks and just breathe in "Jesus! Jesus!" And He is always there!

# Personalizing scripture verses

Another exercise I like to do is to read scripture to God. It really pleases God to hear us speak His Word back to Him. I particularly like to read Psalms and change the words to make it a first person conversation so that I am talking to God.

For example, I especially like to read Psalm 105. I do it like this, "I give thanks to you Lord and call on Your name; I will make known among the nations what You have done. I sing to You, sing praise to You; I tell of Your wonderful acts...You sent Moses Your servant, and Aaron, whom You had chosen. They performed Your miraculous signs among them, Your wonders in the land of Ham...You turned their rain into hail, with lightning throughout their land; You struck down their vines and fig trees and shattered the trees of their country...You brought out Your people with rejoicing, Your chosen ones with shouts of joy; You gave them the lands of the nations, and they fell heir to what others had toiled for – that they might keep Your precepts and observe Your laws. I praise You, Lord." Psalm 105: 1,2,26,27,32,33,43-45.

Reading scripture aloud in itself is a good thing. It helps to both *see* and *hear* the word of God (you know, that repetition thing again). However, there's something amazingly effective and very valuable in the practice of repeating to God the amazing things He has done that builds my faith and confidence in who He is. That is why I particularly like Psalm 105, because it lays out so clearly His faithfulness to the Israelites. I am reminded that He is able to accomplish the things that concern me today.

At first, changing the words around to first person seems a bit awkward, but it gets easier after you've practiced it. If you plan to try this exercise, let me encourage you to keep at it even if at first it seems strange. I am confident that you will love the time you spend worshipping God in this way.

## Journaling

Probably my favorite quiet time exercise is journaling. Some people get journals with pretty fabric covers and colored pages. They might have inspirational quotes or thought provoking questions in them. Personally, I stock up on spiral notebooks when school supplies go on sale. I don't think the medium matters so much (though that's just my personality) as the act of recording on paper the wonders of who God is and what He has done.

I write *everything*. When I am struggling with something, I write about it. When I am rejoicing in something, I write that down, too. When God has given me insights into trials I'm facing, I record them. When I am frustrated because I'm not getting the answers I so desperately need, that goes in there, too. I worship God by telling Him who He is to me. I write out prayers and give praise reports.

I receive many blessings from keeping a journal. One is that writing things out helps me to see things more clearly, often helping me to find solutions to my troubles. Another is that I have developed a habit of looking for evidence of God at work *so that* I can write it down. It makes me more sensitive to His actions.

The blessing for which I am most thankful is I have a record of God's love and faithfulness in my life. I love to sit down on occasion with one of my journals and re-read my entries, thanking God for what He has done.

If you aren't already keeping a journal, please, please consider starting one. Maybe you think you don't have time, or writing has never been "your thing." I am confident, given the chance, you will come to love this exercise and will be so glad you made the effort.

## Author's Note

Well, here we are, at the end of the book but not the end of the journey. I'm so glad you came along with me.

I hope you have been encouraged. I pray that you have confidence knowing, wherever you are and whatever fire you're in, God is there with you and He is doing what is best for you. Beloved, (and you are!) God is good, all the time. He rejoices over you with singing. His thoughts for you are countless as the sands on the seashore. He will never stop doing good to you. When your refining fire seems too hot to handle, remember who God is — too wise to ever make a mistake and too loving to ever do anything unkind — and choose to trust Him. He will never let you down!

If you are so inclined, I would love to hear from you. Visit my web site **www.IrritableMother.com** and drop me a line!

# www.IrritableMother.com

Visit www.IrritableMother.com
to request your free copy of the
— *Irritable Mother's Survival Kit* —

**If you enjoyed reading this book,
you'll love Karen in person.**

She is available for key note addresses or workshops.

Visit www.IrritableMother.com

to schedule Karen to speak to your group.

—

# Chapter Notes

## Part I
[1] Georgius Agricola, *De Re Metallica* (New York: Dover Publications, Inc., 1950), p.1.
[2] Agricola, p.30.
[3] Agricola, p.117, 118.

## Chapter 2
[1] "The Heart of Worship" by Matt Redman, ©ThankYou Music, All Rights Reserved. Used by Permission.
[2] *Expository Dictionary of Bible Words Regency Reference Library* (Grand Rapids, Michigan: The Zondervan Corporation, 1985), p.542.
[3] *New Bible Dictionary* (Downers Grove, Illinois: InterVarsity Press, 2000), p.1058.

## Part II
[1] Georgius Agricola, *De Re Metallica* (New York: Dover Publications, Inc., 1950), p.268-275.
[2] Agricola, p.287-293, 319-321.
[3] Agricola, p.379-382.

## Chapter 3
[1] Jerry Bridges, *Growing Your Faith* (Colorado Springs, Colorado: NavPress, 2004), p.25.
[2] "Here I am to Worship" by Tim Hughes, ©2001 ThankYou Music, All Rights Reserved. Used by Permission.
[3] John 15:13.
[4] Bridges, p.57.

## Chapter 4
[1] Jerry Bridges, *Growing Your Faith* (Colorado Springs, Colorado: NavPress, 2004), p.134.
[2] Bridges, p.120.
[3] Bridges, p.121.
[4] Bridges, p.148.
[5] Bridges, p.152.

## Chapter 5
[1] "Jesus Loves Me" Public Domain.
[2] John Stott, *Romans* (Downers Grove, Illinois InterVarsity Press, 1994), p.82.
[3] Ruth Meyers, *The Satisfied Heart* (Colorado Springs, Colorado: WaterBrook Press, 1999), p.82.

## Part III
[1] Georgius Agricola *De Re Metallica* (New York: Dover Publications, Inc., 1950), p.487.
[2] Agricola, p.485-486.
[3] Agricola, p.487.
[4] For one version of this story, go online to www.scborromeo.org/wisdom/malachi33. htm.

## Chapter 6
[1] "Stubborn Love" by Amy Grant, Brown Bannister, Gary Chapman, Michael W. Smith, Sloan Towner Germann, ©Bases Loaded Music/Meadowgreen Music Company, All Rights Reserved. Used by Permission.

## Chapter 7
[1] "Refiner's Fire" by Brian Doerksen, ©1990 Vineyard Songs (Canada)(Socan) Admin. in North America by Music Services o/b/o Vineyard Music USA. Used By Permission. All Rights Reserved.
[2] ed. A.J. Russell, *God Calling* (Grand Rapids, Michigan: Spire Books published by Jove Publications, Inc. for Fleming H Revell a division of Baker Book House Company), p.74.

## Chapter 8
[1] Ruth Meyers, *31 Days of Praise* (Sisters, Oregon: Multnomah Publishers, Inc., 1994) p.49.

## Chapter 9
[1] Jerry Bridges, *Growing Your Faith* (Colorado Springs, Colorado: NavPress, 2004) p. 148.
[2] Bridges, p.151.
[3] "How Would I Know" by Jacqueline Gouche-Farris, Andrew Winston Gouche, ©1997 by Irving Music, Inc., Jgouche Music, Yo Gouche Music, All rights administered by Irving Music, Inc./BMI. Used By Permission. All Rights Reserved.